The Day the Voices Stopped

The Day the Voices Stopped

{*A Memoir of Madness and Hope*}

KEN STEELE
and
Claire Berman

BASIC
BOOKS

A Member of the Perseus Books Group

Copyright © 2001 by Ken Steele and Claire Berman

Published by Basic Books,
A Member of the Perseus Books Group

Designed by Elliott Beard

Library of Congress Cataloging-in-Publication Data
Steele, Ken, 1948–2000.
    The day the voices stopped : a schizophrenic's journey from madness to hope / Ken Steele with Claire Berman
        p.   cm.
    ISBN 0-465-08227-0
    1. Steele, Ken, 1948–2000.   2. Schizophrenics—
United States—Biography.   I. Berman, Claire.   II. Title.

RC514 .S754   2001
616.89'82'0092—dc21
[B]

                                    00-066739

MV   03 04   10 9 8 7 6 5 4 3

In loving memory of Emma Mae Wilder-White
My grandmother and best friend

"I'm not just managing my illness, I have a real life now."

—*Ken Steele*

CONTENTS

Foreword, by Stephen Goldfinger, M.D.   ix

Prologue   xiii

1   Descent into Madness   1

2   Further into the Abyss   13

3   The Big City   33

4   Welcome to Bedlam   51

5   Caught in the Revolving Door   83

6   Closing Other Doors   119

7   Second Chances   163

8   The Day the Voices Stopped   199

9   Other People's Stories   219

Afterword: What Needs to Be Done   241

Acknowledgments   255

FOREWORD

Ken Steele and I first met in 1981, when he was a homeless, psychotic man living in an alleyway in San Francisco. I have no real memory of that first encounter—Ken was just one of the hundreds of foul-smelling, unshaven, psychologically disorganized men and women I worked with day after day. Most were on the streets, in a desperate exile forced on them by overpowering voices and hallucinations. As a psychiatrist, I did what I could to help, but I faced the depressing reality that many of them would live out their lives in institutions or, worse, return to the streets.

Many years later I was in New York, helping to produce a video on rehabilitation: Ken was also involved in the project, and I was introduced to him again. He struck me as a remarkably intelligent and thoughtful man, so much so that I was alarmed to hear that he had spent decades hospitalized for schizophrenia. I actually suspected that he may have been misdiagnosed. The man before me was smart, funny and an engaging conversationalist—hardly the traits one associates with schizophrenia.

Not long after that, Ken told me he knew me from the past. As he described how we had crossed paths in San Francisco, I was stunned that he had been one of the homeless men I had worked with. He generously thanked me for helping him. It's a rare gift for a psychiatrist to receive such thanks, and it was all the more meaningful coming from someone who had not only survived such profound personal tragedy, but had focused his life on understanding and easing the suffering of others.

American society is beginning to radically alter its view of people with mental illness, thanks in no small measure to Ken's remarkable work as educator, activist and mentor. Ken's intelligence and vision helped make the widely distributed newspaper *New York City Voices*, which he founded and served as editor-in-chief, a strong and articulate tool for empowering and educating the mental health community, especially those, like Ken, who suffer from mental illness themselves.

One of Ken's most dramatic achievements was his creation of the Voter Empowerment Project, a call to arms for those whose mental illnesses had left them disenfranchised and alienated from the political spectrum. By registering 28,000 voters among the mentally ill, Ken assured that mental health issues would gain the attention of politicians and become a visible part of public policy and healthcare debates. Ken's efforts have certainly paid off. In the midst of her senate campaign, Hillary Clinton contributed a Candidate's Statement on Mental Health Issues to *New York City Voices*, in which she praised Ken's "intrepid determination," thanks to which, "the voices of the mentally ill are now beginning to be heard first-hand." What few know is that she also called to solicit his input on mental health issues.

Along with his advocacy, Ken offered extraordinary support and wisdom on a personal level to other sufferers of mental illness and their families. He traveled the country lecturing families on the best ways to support their mentally ill loved ones, using his own painful history as an instructive example. Ken's efforts as a counselor, support group leader, and advisor personally affected thousands of lives.

Ken Steele's personality and accomplishments are extraordinary, but I hope that soon his recovery will become one of the less remarkable aspects of his story. While the effect of the anti-psychotic medication that allowed Ken finally to live without his voices was in many ways miraculous, it is certainly not unique. Although relatively effective medications to treat schizophrenia have been available for several years, for many people these drugs had little, or no, effect. Recently, a new generation of "atypical antipsychotics" has offered new hope to millions of people around the world. In addition to offering improvement to those previously untouched by older medications, they also have fewer side effects than earlier drugs, making it more likely that those for whom they are prescribed will, in fact, take them. We are now seeing many "Rip Van Winkle" cases like Ken's: people re-entering the world after decades of separation.

Ken's portrayal of the fateful "day the voices stopped" is one of the most riveting and provocative scenes I have ever read. In this gripping and startling memoir, Ken Steele reveals his world—the world of severe mental illness—with an intimacy and power few of us would otherwise be privileged to share. Ken is a classic American hero battling adversity, but the impediments he overcomes are within himself. His strength and his foibles, his rage and his courage, and finally his tenacity and dedication force us to confront ourselves and our world in a new light and with a new empathy. This memorable book will enrich the lives of everyone who reads it.

Shortly after Ken's death, Rita Seiden, his final therapist, who helped bring him from years of darkness into light and life, published a tribute to Ken in *New York City Voices*. She wrote: "Everything about you was big—your size, your intelligence, your personality, your drive to make something out of your life after all those wasted years of mental illness, your capacity to bully and exasperate, your ability to convince others that your vision needed to be fulfilled."

Ken, I hope that through this book, and with the support of those who loved and admired you, we can begin to fulfill your vision.

Stephen Mark Goldfinger, M.D.
January 2001
New York

PROLOGUE

"HE IS WELL KNOWN throughout the mental health movement in this country for helping to lead the effort to rewrite how our society views people living with mental illness. . . . He publishes a major newspaper written by and for the consumers of mental health services. He created a highly successful voter empowerment program for the mentally ill. There are many individuals who directly attribute their first steps in recovery to having read about Ken, heard Ken on [the] radio, or seen him on television, . . . who have reached out to him and to whom he has responded. For these achievements, and more, the National Mental Health Association is privileged to present the Clifford W. Beers Award for 1999, our highest honor, to Ken Steele."

The speaker was Joseph Glazer, president and CEO of the Mental Health Association in New York State. I am told that the 400 guests at the association's annual conference, held at

L'Enfant Plaza Hotel in Washington, D.C., that June evening, stood and applauded as I rose to accept the prestigious award. I don't remember that . . . or walking from my seat to the podium . . . or even what I said when I got there. My entire body was trembling. My heart was pounding so hard that I worried I'd collapse before I reached the dais. *You've got to do this, Ken,* I told myself. *It's all right. You're safe here.*

There is a part of me that finds it hard to accept my present situation—that real people, in their true voices, are talking about me and that the things they are saying are complimentary. That's because, for thirty-two years, my world had been ruled by evil, derisive voices that were continually saying derogatory things to and about me. For thirty-two years, these destructive voices inhabited my disordered mind . . . teasing me, mocking me, driving me time and again to the very edge of life . . . and daring me to take the final step.

{1}

Descent into Madness

THE VOICES ARRIVED without warning on an October night in 1962, when I was fourteen years old. *Kill yourself. . . . Set yourself afire,* they said. Only moments before, I'd been listening to a musical group called Frankie Valli and the Four Seasons singing "Walk like a man, fast as I can . . ." on the small radio that sat on the night table beside my bed. But the terrible words I heard now were not the lyrics to that song. I stirred, thinking I was having a nightmare, but I wasn't asleep; and the voices—low and insistent, taunting and ridiculing—continued to speak to me from the radio. *Hang yourself,* they told me. *The world will be better off. You're no good, no good at all.*

Terrified, I turned off the radio, got out of bed, and crept down the hallway in my bare feet, a full harvest moon lighting my way. But the voices would not be tuned out. They accompanied me. *You should die,* muttered one. *You should never have been born,* shrieked another. They were talking to me . . . someone or something wanted *me* to die. Who was doing the talking? What was going on? I turned the handle to the door of my parents' bedroom, looking for safety, but my mom and dad were sleeping soundly, and I was afraid to wake them. I knew they had to go to work in the morning. My parents, Sarah and Kenneth Steele, both had jobs at the Timex plant in Waterbury, Connecticut, not far from the little town of Prospect where we lived. And even if I woke them, what would I say? The voices supplied an answer. *Go right in to him,* they said. *Tell your dad that you're afraid of the dark and then tell him about us. It will only confirm what he already knows—that you're different, a disappointment.*

My father, named Kenneth but called Bud, had wanted a baseball-playing son; I was a boy who read books. I took my first steps dragging along a baseball bat that my father had placed in my hand. Later, I can remember peeing in my pants during a Little League baseball game so that I wouldn't have to play, but Dad forced me to go out on the field in the soiled uniform. Over the years, in ways both stern and subtle, he made it abundantly clear that I had failed him. *He won't believe you.* The voices were right: This was not a man to whom I could confide that I was hearing things.

I wandered down the stairs of our tidy Cape Cod–style house to my grandmother's bedroom. Emma Mae Wilder-White, my mother's mother, was my best friend. I could tell her anything and she would still love me. As I turned the knob to her room, the voices in my head grew shriller and louder until I felt I was drowning in sound. *Die, die, die. You're worthless, no good. Do it now, not later.* I staggered into the living room and collapsed on the floor.

My mother found me lying there in the morning.

"What are you doing up so early?" she asked, shaking my shoulder. I mumbled some sort of answer, something Mom could accept. I remember thinking that my mother had arrived, like a lifeguard, to rescue me and that now I was safe. But my relief was short-lived. The voices were still there, lower in volume and chattering in the singsong cadence that children use to taunt one another. *Na na na na na / We're still he-ere / You thought you got rid of us / No such lu-uck.*

Standing over me in the still-darkened room, my mom was saying, "What are you doing downstairs in your pajamas, Kenny? Have you brushed your teeth? Don't let your father find you like this." There were two sound tracks coming at me at once; I felt bombarded by the noise and terrified by the strangeness of what was happening. *Act normal,* I told myself.

I washed and dressed hurriedly. *Look how ugly you are, look at those blackheads,* the voices taunted as I checked myself out in the bathroom mirror. A familiar face stared back at me: wavy brown hair, eyes that could look either brown or hazel, a longish face that others might have described as handsome. Like most teenagers, I was hypercritical of my appearance. But the voices were even harsher. *You're ugly,* they screamed. *How can you bear to look at yourself?* I went down to breakfast and forced myself to eat. My parents soon left for work, and, as she did every morning, Grandma let me watch the *Today* show, my favorite television program, before I left for school. (Our house was directly across from Algonquin Junior High, and it took only minutes for me to leave one and arrive at the other.)

Barbara Walters and Hugh Downs were co-anchors of the *Today* show in those days. There was a film critic named Judith

Crist, whom I liked, and a newscaster whose name I don't recall. As I sat in front of the TV, all these people began to talk about me. They spoke in borrowed voices, as if their own voices had been dubbed over by actors in a foreign film. *Today, Kenny Steele will kill himself,* roared the newscaster in a voice he might use to warn viewers of a fast-advancing hurricane. An electric shock ran through my body. Had I heard right?

Seconds later, Hugh Downs spoke to me in a deeper voice: *Don't kill yourself, Kenny. Don't give up. Try not to do it.* Barbara Walters conducted a posthumous interview with me. *Why did you kill yourself?* she asked. *Did you really mean to do it?* When it was Judith Crist's turn, the voice that came out of her told me what a fine movie my death would make. The voices were loud and clear. I sat transfixed before the TV set. Then the voices grew low and began whispering about me. *He's listening,* said one. *Well, that's exactly what I want him to do,* answered another. A third voice joined the duo. *Leave home,* this voice demanded with harsh urgency. *These people are no good for you. Leave* now.

I raced out the door. The voices were screaming at me. *Run, run, run, you coward.* I turned right and ran past the school building but did not go in. Instead, I headed for the forest next to the school. I hoped to hide from the voices among the dense foliage, but they found me and continued their diatribe. *You're worthless.... Your parents don't want you around anymore.... You could leave home.... Leave home.... Better yet, you could kill yourself.... Yes, that's it. That's the answer.... Die.* The tall trees became giant question marks. Whose voices were these? Why were they saying such terrible things about me?

I don't know how long I lingered in the forest that day, but I do recall that when I returned home Grandma was clearly upset. She took one look at me, stroked my forehead, and declared, "You're running a temperature, Kenny." It was a fever of 102 degrees, enough to have my mother stay home from work the next day—a rare occasion because her pay would be docked. In a few days, the fever went away and I went back to school. But the voices stayed with me, and I began to struggle to put one foot in front of the other, to make it through each and every day.

A couple of weeks later, on October 22, Dad came home from work excited. "The president will be speaking about the Cuban missile crisis tonight," he said. "I want you to hear what he has to say about the Communists." I joined my father in the living room, and he turned on the TV set. As President Kennedy spoke to the nation, *my* voices spewed obscenities at me. It was impossible for me to hear and understand what was being said about the missile crisis, something that my father clearly cared a great deal about.

The president concluded his talk, and Dad began to speak to me. Here's what I heard:

What are they teaching you in school

> *Don't listen to your father. He's no good.*

about Khruschev and Cuba and about those

> *Don't answer his questions. . . .*

terrible Communists and their plan to ravage the world?"

> *Turn your back on him. . . . Turn away now.*

My father was worried about the looming international crisis, and he wanted to make sure I was learning the right things, but I was drowning in these cacophonous sounds and couldn't answer him. I felt powerless to pull myself to safety. In response to his barrage of questions, I mumbled, "What?" and "I don't know." Dad knew I wasn't ignorant, so he decided I was being willful. What happened next only confirmed that belief.

Whenever I was near a television set or radio, the voices grew louder and more intense, and there seemed to be more of them. It was as if they were writing and directing the story of my life, telling me what I could and could not do, leaving little room for improvisation. That evening, the voices won out. As my father quizzed me about what we had seen on TV, what I knew, what I thought, I did as the voices directed: I put my hands over my ears and turned my back to him.

Dad became enraged. "Go to bed without dinner," he ordered me, stalking out of the living room. It was a punishment he rarely imposed. *Ungrateful boy,* now *see what you've done,* said my voices. *You have disappointed your father one more time. Your parents deserve a better son than you.*

Soon they would have one. Some time after the voices first visited me, my mother and father told me they were expecting a baby. They had tried for years to have another child, had even declared several pregnancies that turned out to be false, but this pregnancy was apparently the real thing. I did not share their joy. An only child for close to fifteen years, I wasn't eager to welcome a rival for their attention and affections. *If I have to have a sibling,* I prayed, *let it be a sister.*

But the voices knew better. They had decided the baby would be a boy, and on several terrifying occasions they made it seem as if "he" were speaking to me. *I am coming, I'm going to be born,* my soon-to-be brother would whisper menacingly from inside my mother's swollen stomach. *You have to leave.* Soon other voices would join in—a deafening chorus that dictated ways in which I might manage my leave-taking: *Take a radio into the bathtub and electrocute yourself. . . . Jump in front of a car at night on Route 69. . . . Pour charcoal lighter fluid over your body and set yourself afire. . . . Hang yourself in the forest.* They would provide precise instructions on how to perform these suicides, and I would listen, riveted by their sounds and sights—for by now I was also being visited by strange images: indistinct shapes that swayed before my mind's eye.

At times, the images would appear more clearly, but only for split seconds, like a camera shutter opening and closing so quickly that I couldn't recognize what I was being shown. These visual images came and went, but the voices were with me always—sometimes roaring in my ears, sometimes chattering in the background. Increasingly, I found myself inclined to obey their commands.

My brother, Joseph Robert Steele, was born on May 10, 1964. The fact that the voices had correctly determined his sex gave them a lot of credibility. *He's here now,* they said, laughing maniacally. *Joey is the good son. . . . He's the one they wanted. . . . Wait and see, Joey will be a professional baseball player.* (In fact, when Joe grew up, he came quite close to playing ball professionally.) *Your dad will love him more, and he'll deserve it. . . . It's time for you to go. . . . Stop hanging around.*

Only two things, reading and writing, could tone the voices down. When I read, I entered the world of David Copperfield or Huckleberry Finn; I'd suffer the growing pains of

Holden Caulfield or the agonies of Oliver Twist. The voices would then become muffled, like a radio playing in the background. And so I read voraciously. I read everything I could get my hands on, while the voices waited in the wings, ready to surge onto the stage as soon as I turned the last page. We had a set of the *World Book Encyclopedia,* and I read all the volumes, some of them two or three times. I read my way through the last year of junior high school and wrote frantically, scribbling page after page of homework, trying to finish before the voices took over. Amazingly, I graduated from junior high with honors.

By graduation, however, I had separated myself from most of my friends. *See, even your friends don't like you anymore,* the voices told me. *See how they look at you? Strange . . . Look at Johnny. He used to be your best friend. He's out to get you now.*

More and more, I stayed at home, afraid to ride my bike in the street. Who knew what dangers lurked beyond the door of my home? Still, I managed to cover up what was happening to me, or so I thought. For the first three years, I *was* at times able to function in both the event world (get up, go to school, help take care of the baby) and my hallucinatory world, but I walked a thin wire. Grandma would overhear me responding out loud to the voices' demands and think I was on the phone with a friend. Apparently, she hadn't noted that my schoolmates no longer called or came by. "Kenny, you know your parents want you to keep the phone free," she'd call out, reminding me of the house rules. Her voice would bring me back to reality. "Sorry, Grandma," I'd say, and I'd walk into the kitchen where she was preparing dinner, trying to stay calm, to show her that all was well.

But all was far from well. The voices were stepping up their demands that I destroy myself. *No simple death for you,* they railed. *Guts and gore and a big mess . . . that's the way you must take your life.* Sometimes, they would start whispering, as if they were plotting against me, and I had to strain to hear them, or they would imitate monks performing a Gregorian chant, speaking to me in the Latin that was then still used in the celebration of the Roman Catholic mass. Then they would warn me, *Remember, Kenny, you cannot be forgiven your sins when you commit suicide.* The message was clear: I would die, but I'd fail to achieve grace.

Day after day, I flailed about in an ocean of sound so overwhelming that I would sometimes find myself capitulating to the voices' demands. "Okay, I'll kill myself," I would tell them. Anything . . . if they would only let me be for a while. I was a perpetual guest at a noisy party, seeking a quiet corner, vainly trying to bargain for just a little peace.

"Okay, I'll set myself on fire. . . . I'll hang myself. Yes, yes, I'll kill myself." It was August. Only when I heard my mother scream and felt my father shaking me into consciousness did I realize that I had blurted out those words in the living room in front of my entire family. The voices told me what I needed to do then. *No more hiding. Your family knows everything now,* they said. *You've got to escape. . . . Get out that door. . . . Run, run, run. You've got to die.*

And so I ran away from home. I ran to the same forest in which I had sought refuge the first time the voices had descended on me. It was black under the white birches, maples, and pine trees, their stinging branches as dark as my fear. In the forest, the voices took over completely, but— strangely—they also seemed softer, more consoling. *It's really not your fault. You didn't bring this on yourself, you know.* Still, their message was the same: *You have to die.*

Over the last several months, this message had become more potent, for the voices had offered to help, even giving me explicit instructions. *Get a rope,* they ordered me, *twelve feet long and two inches thick.* I'd gone to a hardware store and bought the rope. *Tie the noose with a sea knot, and make sure it's tied tight,* the voices said, but they hadn't told me how to make the knot. One day at school, I approached a fellow Boy Scout, someone who had done knot-tying to earn one of his badges. "How can I learn to tie a sea knot?" I asked him. He gave me the name of an instruction manual, an old New England primer with drawings of tall ships, that provided illustrated, step-by-step directions on how to tie knots, how to expand the size of a loop, how to make sure the knot would not come out. I'd found a copy of the book in the town library, and I practiced tying knots.

At the direction of the voices, I had also taken a step stool from the basement and hidden it in the forest, covering it over with branches and leaves. I'd bought lighter fluid and matches and left them in a small locker that I'd hidden in the same area. When all the preparations had been made, the voices were pleased with me. *Good, your suicide kit is complete,* they said.

That night—the night I ran away—I made three different attempts on my life. First, I got up on the stool, then tied the noose around my neck. But even though I tossed and thrashed about, I couldn't manage to kick the stool away. I had failed, and the voices made much of this. *You weren't able to do this simple thing,* they said. *You're not man enough.* They called me things like *sissy* and *faggot.* They called me a sow. *You're a fucking pig,* they said. I got down from the stool. Then the voices turned into a wave of sound so strong, I felt as if I'd been physically knocked down by their force. Tears streaming down my face, I located the charcoal lighter fluid and poured it on my head. I could not bring myself to light a match.

The highway, I thought, half running, half dragging myself in my disoriented state about a mile to Route 69, a well-traveled road that connects Waterbury to New Haven, Connecticut. My plan was to leap in front of a car. I stood at the side of the road. Headlights were coming at me. *Now,* I told myself, but just then I noticed a spotlight atop the car. What if this was a state police car? What if the police were coming for me? Panicked, I ran back from the road, back toward the school that sat dark and deserted in the summer night. I crouched behind the building, clinging to its hard concrete walls for what seemed like eternity. After a while, I went back to the forest and fell asleep.

The following morning, I rose and headed for home. My parents' cars were in the driveway. *It must be the weekend or a holiday,* I figured; that's why their cars were there. It never occurred to me that my mom and dad were home because of the events of the previous night. Two state trooper cars were parked outside our house. Dad stood in our front yard, talking animatedly with the troopers. *They're going to shoot you. See the guns in their holsters? Your dad is arranging to have you killed.* I froze in my tracks. My dad turned and saw me.

My parents had called the troopers, reporting me as a runaway who had threatened suicide. Now the officers wanted to escort me to the hospital for observation. Dad convinced them to let him take me to our family physician, Dr.

Sullivan, instead. He phoned the doctor, who agreed to see me at the end of the day.

It was growing dark and pouring when we drove up to keep the appointment. The doctor's office was in a three-story building with a large porch that ran almost its full length. Only a few windows on the first floor were lit. The other physicians who shared the suite of medical offices had gone home.

After letting us in, Dr. Sullivan asked my parents if he could speak with me alone. I have no memory of what the doctor said or did, but I clearly recall the looks of worry and confusion on my parents' faces when the doctor called them back in and spoke with them. I remember the expression on my strong father's face. I had never seen it before. It was a look of total defeat.

Mom, Dad, and I returned home. Later that night, I heard my father speaking on the telephone. He was talking about me. He was telling the person on the other end that I had a very serious mental illness. It had a long name, and I remember wanting to know how to spell it. That way, I could look it up in the library—like finding out how to make a sea knot—and learn how to deal with the illness, how to get rid of the voices and all the crazy ideas and thoughts that had been swirling in my mind.

I walked over to my dad and asked him if he would spell the disease that Dr. Sullivan said I was suffering from. Dad leaned his forehead into his left hand and handed me a small slip of paper that he held in his right hand. On it, there was one word, neatly printed in capital letters:

SCHIZOPHRENIA

{ 2 }

Further into the Abyss

OSSING AND TURNING that night, I waited impatiently for morning to come. I kept checking the clock on the radio that sat beside my bed. *Five o'clock*. Just five more hours until the library opened. *Six o'clock*. Four hours to go. . . . I could not rest without knowing what was really wrong with me. *Seven o'clock*. I rose as if getting ready for a regular day, then went through the motions of washing, dressing, eating, without any idea of what I was wearing, what I put into my mouth. I mumbled something about going to see a friend, ran out the front door, and headed for the library

The slip of paper that my dad had given me lay crumpled in my pants pocket. Waiting for the library to open, I took it out, straightened it, read the word written on it, replaced the paper in my pocket, then took it out again. Time never seemed so slow. Finally, the doors opened. Once inside the building, I asked Virginia, the librarian, where I could find a medical dictionary. She pointed toward a reference shelf at the rear of the room. I hurried over, took down a thick, black-covered volume, riffled through its pages, and quickly found what I was looking for:

Schizo·phre·nia: a psychotic disorder characterized by withdrawal from reality, delusions, hallucinations, and disintegration of the personality. Includes some form of insanity and dementia praecox.

Insanity! I returned to the information desk and, in a small voice, asked Virginia to give me everything else she had on the subject.

I waited tensely while she sought to fill my request. My thoughts raced from one word, *delusions*, to another, *hallucinations*. My stomach was churning. Was this what it was like to be insane? Virginia brought me a pile of heavy books from the reference collection, and I muddled through them. The news was not good. I had hoped to discover scientific facts and some direction—a way to deal with the awful things that were happening to me. Instead, I found conjecture and confusion.

As best I could gather, the cause of this illness was little known or understood. The words that stayed with me from the descriptions I read next to the word *schizophrenia* were "incurable" and "lifelong." There was mention of violence, which scared me. There were case studies of people who killed others, as well as histories of people who killed themselves after their imaginary voices told them to do it. As I read about suicide, it felt like the voices were reading to me—they were that close, that insistent. My chest tightened and sweat covered my brow as I pictured myself dying and people attending my funeral. And if I lived? I read that they locked up people with schizophrenia and threw away the keys. I shoved the books across the library table; I desperately needed to put space between me and the terrifying message they contained.

Today I would define *schizophrenia* differently, as a biological brain disorder that is manageable if properly treated with medication and psychotherapy, along with peer and/or family support. I would put much less emphasis on violence against others. Less than 1 percent of people with schizophrenia ever become violent; in fact, they are more likely to have violence committed against them. Although schizophrenia remains a great mystery, I and others who know this illness through personal experience or as mental health professionals would sound a note of hope. We know today that much *can* be done to help people not only survive schizophrenia, but have a life, as I do now. But four decades ago, alone at a table in my small-town library, the message I received was of despair, not hope.

As soon as I stopped reading, the voices turned the volume up. *You were a mistake,* they taunted me. *Your mom and dad want you out of their lives. Your grandmother doesn't want you around, either.* The voices were relentless. I sat in the library for hours, delaying for as long as possible my return to a home where (if the voices were to be believed) I was no longer welcome.

If home was unsafe, the world outside was even more dangerous.

Gradually, I began to believe the voices' message: that *everyone* wanted me gone—everyone, that is, but my grandmother.

The voices had her on my enemies list, but I knew better. If anybody could help me out of my terror, she could. One August afternoon in 1963, Grandma sat sewing at the kitchen table, her yellow canary singing in a cage behind her. The summer sun shone through the window, highlighting Grandma's soft, white hair, which she wore pulled back in a bun, loose tendrils framing her face. It was a tranquil scene, soon to be disturbed. I summoned up the courage to confide in her.

"Grandma," I said, "people are talking about me."

"What people?" she asked, not looking up from her work.

"The neighbors," I began. My plan was to lead up slowly to the fact that I was hearing voices.

"That's what neighbors are for," Grandma replied flatly, not missing a stitch. "They gossip."

Then, stammering in fear and embarrassment, I told my grandmother about the voices—about how they'd first visited me, how they shouted obscenities at me, how they constantly directed me to end my life. Haltingly, I described how I'd almost killed myself in the forest.

Grandma put her needle down and looked at me for a very long time. Finally, she rose, went to her bedroom, and returned with her Bible—the same Bible that now has an honored place in my home. She thumbed its well-worn pages, located the passage she'd been looking for, and recited to me from 1 Peter, chapter 5, line 8: "'Be sober, be vigilant; because your adversary the devil, as a roaring lion, walketh about, seeking whom he may devour.'" Grandma had been raised as a Baptist, and for her the voices were obviously the devil at work inside me.

As frightening as this idea was, I believed my grandmother. Her explanation for my illness became my new defi-
nition of schizophrenia; it was the devil working within me.
He was my master now, and I was his child. It was a relationship that terrified me. I spent one sleepless night after
another fighting the voices. Now that I knew they were the
devil's messengers, ordered to torment me, I would do battle
with them. On those summer nights so long ago, I never
dreamed that the war would wage on for decades.

I desperately needed to find a place of sanctuary. My
hometown parish felt off-limits so, a couple of days later, I
hitchhiked to Waterbury, seven miles away, to attend morning mass at Immaculate Conception, a large Roman Catholic
church on West Main Street in the downtown area. I walked
up the church steps, entered, gazed up at the huge, domed
ceiling—at the stained-glass panels framed in gold leaf—and
took a seat near the front of the church, closer to the altar
than I'd ever been. No more than ten people were in attendance that morning. Soon a vested priest appeared, walked
directly to the altar, and genuflected before it. Making the
sign of the cross, he began to chant the Latin prayer, *"In
nomine Patris, et Filii, et Spiritus sancti . . . Amen."*

The voice of the priest was immediately joined by the
chorus of voices residing in my head. *In the name of the
Father and the Son and the Holy Spirit, Kenny thinks he can get
rid of us,* they jeered. Then, ominously: *You will* never *be rid
of us, Kenny. Never, never.*

*"Indulgentiam, absolutionem, et remissionem peccatorum
nostrorum, tribuat nobis, omnipotens et misericors Dominus,"*
recited the priest. (May the almighty and merciful Lord grant
us pardon, absolution, and remission of our sins.) But there

was to be no absolution for me, the voices made clear, for I was commanded to commit suicide—an unpardonable sin. *No pardon,* said one voice. *No absolution,* added another. *There will be no remission of your sins,* declared a third.

In my delusional state, the ten men and women at prayer in the church that morning swelled to a congregation that included my family, school friends, and even strangers, all of whom were glaring at me with contempt, anger, hatred. *Stare back into those eyes,* the voices said. *See, your enemies are everywhere around you. They know you are damned to hell. Go, do their bidding. Die.* I managed to pull myself to my feet, stagger up the aisle, leave the church, and—I don't know how—make it safely back home. But I returned to the church the next day . . . and the next.

That fall, I entered Wilby High School in Waterbury, within easy walking distance of Immaculate Conception. Attending early-morning mass became a weekday ritual, and each time the experience was almost an exact replica of my first visit. These demon voices were dragging me against my will to some other place—some dark, sinister, forbidden place where only those beyond redemption exist.

I was desperate to be rescued. Arriving early at church one morning, I lit candles in front of the statue of the Blessed Virgin and prayed for salvation. I had not accepted the Sacrament since being visited by the voices. Confirmed as a Catholic a year earlier, I had violated God's laws by failing to receive the Body and Blood of Jesus Christ. If I atoned for my sins, might God not be pleased? Might He not cause my voice-demons to go away? They were with me as I lit the candles, mocking me even as I mouthed words of prayer and supplication. We were all in an ancient court, and they were the courtiers—whispering, plotting, scheming to do away with me. In a bold attempt to thwart the conspiracy, I looked about for a priest.

My courage paid off as a priest knelt beside me. In a whisper—with the voices screaming *NO!* in my head—I turned and asked, "Father, will you hear my confession?" He agreed to meet with me after mass.

As I moved toward the confessional, the volume of the voices rose to an almost unbearable pitch. From the part of my mind where they held court, they spoke about me—*Who is he to think the Holy Trinity will pay him any attention?*—and then began shouting obscenities that echoed through my head. Suddenly, they cut off, and one deep, commanding voice took over. *Now see what you've done,* it said, sounding disappointed in me. This was the first time I heard that particular voice, but it wasn't to be the last. I came to think of this voice as The Ruler of my evil court, who was called upon to speak to me only after the courtiers proved ineffective. Sometimes, he would scold the courtiers. I didn't hear The Ruler often, but I always recognized him when he came. Sometimes, he—and he alone—would be with me for days. Over the years of my madness, it was The Ruler who ordered me, with an authority that demanded obedience, to die. Now, entering the confessional, I heard his one solitary bass voice gravely ask, *You think you can be forgiven, do you?* Then came the pronouncement: *You cannot be forgiven.*

Summoning whatever strength was still left to me, I bared my secrets to the priest, Father Bruce Burbank. I told him everything: about the devil voices mocking God and telling me I was no good. I told him that they said my parents no longer wanted me. I told him about the conspiracy against me by friends and neighbors. I told him that the voices repeatedly demanded I end my life by hanging, fire, electrocution . . . that they were saying terrible things to me here and now in the confessional even as I was speaking.

Above the din of the voices, I heard the priest ask if I wished to be absolved and to have salutary penance imposed. I accepted the penance willingly, hopefully, prayerfully. Again I heard the priest's voice, now in Latin: *"Misereatur tui omnipotens Deus, et dismissis peccatis tuis, perducat te ad vitam aeternam. Amen."* (May almighty God have mercy on you, forgive you your sins, and bring you life everlasting. Amen.)

As I left the booth, I was surprised to see the priest emerge from his side. He engaged me in conversation: How old was I? Where did I go to school? What were my favorite subjects? In fact, he was holding me for the police. Fearing that I might take my life, the priest had signaled to one of the church workers while I was at confession and asked him to contact the authorities. Two police officers entered the church. They suggested that we take a ride to St. Mary's Hospital. They didn't seem at all threatening. I went with them quietly.

I was about to have my first meeting with a psychiatrist.

St. Mary's Hospital in Waterbury is where I was born. Over the years, I'd spent time there, waiting in the children's room under the watchful eyes of the nuns while older family members visited ailing relatives. I could gauge the seriousness of the illness by the atmosphere in the car on the trip home. If the relative was on the verge of death, we'd ride back in complete silence. Far more often, the car would be filled with gossip of how this or that aunt or uncle didn't take care of themselves and a whole lot of complaining by my family about having had to listen to the patient's recital of aches and pains.

This visit to St. Mary's was different.

Instead of pulling up in the family car, a 1947 dark blue Plymouth Savoy, I arrived at the hospital in a black-and-white police car. Instead of the nuns who had always been concerned for my safety, two uniformed police officers now stood guard over me. Instead of the waiting room, I was steered to the emergency room where, in a maze of antiseptic white bedsheets, separate areas had been cordoned off to create privacy—or confinement. I felt trapped by the walls of linen, by the police guards stationed outside the enclosure.

"Take off all your clothes, and put this on so that it opens in the rear," said an attendant, handing me a smock. I did as I was told. My buttocks were exposed. I dropped my clothes on a folding chair and remained standing, backed against an examining table and wondering what was going on. *Shame on you,* said the low voice of The Ruler. I feared he would get back at me for bringing him to this alien place.

A man entered the cubicle. He was tall and not very old. "This is Dr. Blackstone," said a nurse, introducing the psychiatrist who'd been summoned to meet me. The doctor asked me a lot of questions: "Do you know where you are? . . . Can you tell me the name of the president of the United States? . . . Can you explain the meaning of the sentence 'A rolling stone gathers no moss'? . . . What is meant by the statement 'People who live in glass houses shouldn't throw stones'?" I stared at the doctor without answering. Nothing he said made any sense to me. This was stupid. *He* was stupid, I told him, clutching my fluttering garment from behind and pulling myself up on the examining table. It was the first time I remember showing disrespect for authority. There were to be many other such occasions.

I heard my father's voice. "Kenny!"

"Dad, I'm here."

I jumped from the table, ran past the doctor, pushed aside the hanging sheets, located my father, and, in a jumble of words, tried to explain all that had been happening to me. The voices had their say as well. *The old man knows you're no good, Kenny boy. . . . Don't expect any meddlesome priests, policemen, or doctors to save you. . . . They know you're no good, too. Do everyone a favor and die now. Die in the hospital. A lot of people do it, you know.* Which of us was my father hearing—me or my voices?

But now Dad was doing the talking. "He's my son and you have no right to hold him here," he told the people who were gathered about me—police, psychiatrist, and Father Burbank, who had arrived sometime during my examination.

My father was not an easy man to stand up to, but Father Burbank tried. "Your son expressed suicidal thoughts," he told my father. "He told me of strange voices ordering him to hurt himself. He needs to be evaluated in a hospital."

"Enough!" my father said, cutting off the priest. He turned to the police officers: "Do I need to post a bond or something?" The officers looked first to each other, then to the psychiatrist.

"No, your son hasn't committed any crime," Dr. Blackstone told my father, adding, "Mr. Steele, we'd like to send Kenneth to Connecticut Valley State Hospital's adolescent unit for an evaluation."

"Nothing doing," said my father.

"Kenneth shared some very worrisome thoughts with Father Burbank," the doctor said. "I'm willing to release the boy to you if you assure me you will have him seen by a psychiatrist."

"I will," said my father in a tone that I recognized as meaning he'd do nothing of the sort. Then he ordered, "Someone get my son's clothes so he can get dressed and we can get out of here." The nurse scurried to do his bidding.

Father Burbank would not be easily dismissed. "Shouldn't you have Mr. Steele sign a release form to protect St. Mary's Hospital from liability if he doesn't have his son examined as promised?" he asked the doctor.

"Are you calling me a liar, Father?" demanded my father. I almost expected him to say, "Let's step outside."

"No, no, Mr. Steele," said Dr. Blackstone, quickly moving between the two men. "We don't need you to sign anything. Father Burbank is just concerned for your boy's welfare, as we know you are, too. Here, let me write down the names of several adolescent psychiatrists you might call." He wrote quickly, handing the list to my father, who put it in his pocket.

The sun was setting when my father and I left the hospital. Nothing was said on the drive home. I recognized the silence; it was the same as when we returned from a visit to a dying family member, confirming my deepest fears that my illness was terminal. Dad was busy with his thoughts, I suppose. I was occupied by my voices—a constant murmur of rejection and recrimination. This time, they were right. No question, I had botched absolution.

That night, as Dad parked the car and we climbed the stairs to the living quarters of our home, I knew that something important had taken place: The insidious process of denying that I had a serious, life-threatening mental illness had begun. This condition of denial would take a strong hold on my family. My mental illness became the elephant in the living room—unmistakably present, yet totally ignored.

For a time, I played into this fantasy. I got up, went to school, came home, and even attempted to do my homework, creating a semblance of normality for those who were satisfied with surface impressions. But the transition from Algonquin Junior High to Wilby High School was not just bumpy, it was cataclysmic.

See her? You know that girl . . . she's your enemy, the voices warned me as I searched my new homeroom for a familiar face and saw Kathy. We'd competed for top grades throughout elementary and junior high school, and our rivalry had been friendly, marked by mutual respect. *She's looking at you. She wants you to die.* And so I avoided Kathy . . . and everyone else who had once been my friend.

The voices that had first visited me came from radio and television personalities, people I'd never met. Now they spoke to me through real people. *Kenneth Steele, why don't you kill yourself,* my homeroom teacher would say when she called the attendance roll each morning. *Try hanging yourself in the boys' bathroom. The pass is at the door.*

You're not dead yet? We're waiting, the assistant principal would taunt as he passed me in the hall. I took to walking close to the walls, slinking my way between classes.

In my hallucinatory world, the science teacher would spend entire sessions explaining to me and my classmates why she thought it would be a good idea to dissect me: *His death would be a good thing . . . this poor creature deserves to*

24

die, and think what we would learn about the insides of an evil one. The day she began to provide precise instructions on *how* to dissect Kenneth Steele, I ran from the room, knocking over books and a student who stood between me and the door. That incident put me back in the world of the white sheets at St. Mary's Hospital; and once again, my father arrived and convinced the doctors that he could handle me. Again we rode home in silence.

That evening from my room, I could hear my father raving. "It's not our fault, I know that," he told my mother in an agitated voice. I could practically feel him pacing back and forth.

"They'll say we didn't raise him right," said my mother.

"What do they know, anyway?" came my father's gruff reply. "We just won't listen to any nonsense."

I knew that the genesis of my illness *was* a question of concern to my parents—and not without reason. More than three decades later, people still tend to blame parents for their children's abnormal behavior. And what I had was abnormal with a capital *A*. If a child is stricken with pneumonia or diabetes, no one points an accusing finger at the parents and says, "You're at fault; you did it." But when a young person comes down with mental illness, people start buzzing: "It must have been in the family" or "We always suspected that there was something strange about them."

What I read about schizophrenia that first day in the library—and much of what I've seen since—placed a lot of blame on parents, especially mothers. I remember reading the phrase *refrigerator mother,* used to describe a woman who was very cold toward her child. My mother was not so much cold as uninvolved. She went to her job on the assembly line at Timex every day, catered to my father's needs at home, and left the raising of me to Grandma. She'd been eighteen years old when she married; my father was nineteen. They were kids, too young to take on the responsibility of raising another kid. As a child, I never really knew my mother. I still don't.

How I wish my parents had known what I would learn decades later: that there's no one to blame for this illness. I tend to accept the generally held belief that schizophrenia runs in families. When I queried my mother (years later) about whether any relatives had been mentally ill, she said, "Not really," then paused and recalled a great aunt who "was constantly speaking to Jesus." Later, another skeleton or two emerged from the family closet. But even if schizophrenia *is* genetically transmitted, the genes would be like the water that freezes in a rock in the winter and breaks it apart. My parents would be no more to blame than the water when the rock shatters. They were simply there, a part of me. And though I often wished they'd been warmer and more accepting of me, I never viewed their parenting style as responsible for my condition.

No matter the reasons, I was falling to pieces before everyone's eyes.

I had been a model student. Now I began to fail in my studies, often skipping school and going instead to where the voices directed. One day, my classmate Kathy trapped me in the hallway outside of my homeroom class, grabbed me by the shoulders, and shook me. "What is *wrong* with you, Ken?" she demanded to know. "Why are you failing everything? You're not studying." She was upset that I was getting D's and F's. "You look terrible and you even smell," she went on. "You're not the person I knew a year ago." Kathy had gone to the teachers, who were writing me off as a bad kid, and had pleaded with them to please look at my record. I pushed her away. She was trying to help me, but her grabbing me like that only made me paranoid about her. Like everyone else, she was out to get me.

Today I understand that a significant change in grades—from really good to really bad—is an early sign that a kid is in trouble. I know, too, that timely intervention can make a difference. But the solution my teachers and parents arrived at was to have me transferred to a different school. It did no good. There is no geographical cure for being sick like this. "He has a mind broken beyond repair," my parents were told time and again by Dr. Sullivan, the first person to diagnose my condition as paranoid schizophrenia. "There's only one treatment for this illness: long-term care in a state institution." My parents' reaction was to leave Dr. Sullivan, who had been our family's physician for many years. Only Grandma continued to see him.

When I turned sixteen, my father and mother allowed me to drop out of school. They hoped I would enroll in a high school correspondence course. Instead, I spent my days at home with my grandmother and baby brother. I stayed in my room most of the time, reading and listening to the radio. (I now tell families that isolation is one of the most common symptoms of this illness and that they need to pay attention to it.) I had no reason to leave my room. I had a whole cast of characters in my head that was keeping me quite busy right there.

During those early years of the illness, I could still move back and forth between my two worlds. One world was "reality": my room, Grandma, my parents; the other world was more real to me . . . and more compelling. I was like an underwater creature that still had the ability to survive on land from time to time. The deeper I got under the water—the more hours each day I spent hallucinating—the more difficult it was to live on land. I sank deeper and deeper into a netherworld, where the voices took over.

For more than a year, I was terrified to go outside to get the mail because of my paranoia. My heart would pound, sweat would pour down my face at the very thought of walking out the front door. I would peek from behind the drawn blinds of my room, obsessively scrutinizing the cars and people who passed by. My mind was filled with lurid scenarios of how they would rush in and then kidnap, torture, or murder me.

Sometimes, I would make myself venture forth in the dark, where I'd sit on the front steps, breathing the night air. But the sweep of a car's headlights, the rustle of leaves would send me instantly to hide at the side of the house. When I thought the coast was clear, I would sneak back inside. But I didn't feel safe there, either. My voices were telling me that something terrible was going to happen, that there were demons all around.

In the underwater world where I was drowning, I saw my father as the biggest demon of all. Our relationship had decayed to a point where we could no longer be in the same room or under the same roof. I feared that he'd catch me speaking to my voices, which was happening more and more frequently. I think he believed that I would do something strange enough to force him to acknowledge that I was not just willful, but sick—an admission he still finds hard to make. There was so much tension between us, I knew I had to get away.

Reading and writing continued to be the only activities in my life that provided respite from the voices. When I would focus on the stories I read or the entries I wrote in my journal, the concentration would tone down the voices and, once in a while, even manage to silence them. One day, reading a New York City arts magazine, I came across an advertisement seeking student writers for the Showcase Theater Company and School in Manhattan. On impulse, I wrote an impassioned letter to the director, whose name was listed in the ad. Shortly thereafter (or so it seemed to me, who no longer had any concept of time), I received a reply. The letter said that I was talented and that I was accepted into the program.

I was seventeen, about the age when a young adult— certainly someone who was not attending school—was expected to get a job and earn his way. My father had already warned me, "When you turn eighteen, any obligations your mother and I have to you are over." The best I could have hoped for if I stayed at home would have been a job at the Timex plant or one of the other factories in the area—something I was determined to avoid. The move to New York presented an alternative that my parents could not just accept, but welcome. I know they were relieved at the idea of my leaving home.

They asked that I delay my departure until after the Christmas holidays. On January 2, 1966, a rainy Sunday, I said good-bye to my grandma, mother, and baby brother, Joey. Hiding my tears, I bent down to pick up my new mini-trunk—a Christmas gift to me that my parents had bought at

Woolworth's—and carried it to the backseat of the car. My father lifted my other piece of luggage—a well-worn suitcase that had previously belonged to his younger brother, Bruce. "You'll make a difference out there," Uncle Bruce had said when he gave me the suitcase. "Different people like you always do." I think he meant to wish me well, but in my paranoid state all I could think was, *What does he mean, I'm "different"?* I remember thinking, *What does he see? What does he know about me?* For me the suitcase was tainted.

During the tense hour-long ride along Route 69 from Prospect into New Haven, where I would take the Hartford–New Haven–New York Railroad, my father muttered, "Well, since you refused to go to school here (playing dumb, which we all know isn't true) and you wouldn't take a job in a factory, you'd be leaving home soon, anyway. You'll probably still end up in the army to fight in Vietnam."

He might just as well have said that I'd go to the moon. Because the voices continued to speak to me from the television set, I didn't follow the news on TV and knew little about our military engagement in a distant land called Vietnam. It just didn't relate to *me* and to the private war that I was waging every day, hour, minute: Ken Steele vs. The Demons.

I heard my father's words, but he seemed to be speaking more to himself than to me—as if he were trying to reassure himself that he was doing the right thing in letting me go. In discharging his parental responsibilities, my father had cashed in a life insurance policy he had set aside for me. He now gave me some of that money and told me he would send the rest as an allowance, in monthly installments. "If you can afford to live and go to that writing school, too, that's your business," he said as we parted.

With those words as a blessing, I boarded the train.

The voices had accomplished what they'd set out to do from the very first day they visited me. They had separated me from my family.

{3}

The Big City

NOW YOU ARE ALL ALONE, except for us. . . . No one at home wants you back. There has been a death in your family, Kenny; it is you. In the big city, you can jump from buildings so high they touch the sky. Imagine the mess you'll make when you hit the street. Climb a tall building, Kenny. Then fly and die. We'll help . . . we'll help . . . we'll help. No one else cares. We'll help.

Cowering in my seat on the train, I believed that the voices were right, that I was hurtling toward my death in a place I did not know. Though New York City was only two hours from New Haven by train, I had never been there. There was some talk in our family of visiting New York during the summer of 1964 to attend the World's Fair, and I remember being cautiously excited at the prospect—wanting to go, yet afraid to venture forth—but somehow our plans were changed. Instead, we traveled to Pittsburgh to see my father's favorite team, the Pirates, play baseball. Now, as the train bumped and sped along the tracks, quickly taking me away to a fabled Oz where I prayed that my wish for safety would be granted, the voices seized on my panic. *We're all you have, Kenny. Sooner or later, you will have to do our bidding. Make it sooner.*

I buried my head in the help-wanted section of the New York newspaper that my father had handed me before he left. Employment agencies offered all sorts of publishing jobs, including some for beginners. I circled the names of several agencies, planning to visit them first thing the next morning. And then a curious thing happened: Though the voices were still jabbering at me, for the first time in a long while I felt a sense of hope. Something about making plans helped me get hold of myself, giving me courage to meet the challenges that lay immediately ahead.

Nothing, however, had prepared me for Grand Central Station. The main concourse, one of the grandest rooms ever built in America—120 feet wide, 375 feet long—was surmounted by a vaulted ceiling studded with electric stars. Against one wall, a Kodak exhibit showed a picture of happy children celebrating the holidays in a warm family setting. How very different this scene was from the dismal time our family had just spent "celebrating" the holidays, pretending that ours was a normal, happy family.

Loudspeakers blared. People rushed to catch departing trains and meet arriving passengers. The redcap who had helped me with my luggage asked if I needed a cab. "I don't have money for a cab," I said.

He looked at me, probably dismissing any chance for a tip, and said, "See that word *strike* on the front page of your newspaper, son? There's a shutdown going on. The subways and buses are not running. How far you goin'?"

I'd reserved a room at the YMCA Sloane House on West Thirty-fourth Street between Eighth and Ninth Avenues, eight streets south and many blocks west of Grand Central. "You're not gonna be able to tote all this stuff by yourself," said the redcap. He directed me to a locker, where I stored the trunk, inserting enough coins in the slot to buy time until the following afternoon. Above the roar of the people, trains, loudspeakers, the voices in my head shouted to be heard. *Little boy swallowed up by the big city,* they said. *Lost, lost, you're losing it, Kenny. This is your crypt. You will lie here when you die.* I found myself paralyzed by fear and confusion. I looked about the concourse. Which way was out?

There I stood—a teenager six feet tall, 150 pounds, wearing pants that were too short and carrying a worn suitcase. I looked very much alone and exposed. A man approached. He reminded me of one of my junior high school teachers: tall, slim, in his early thirties. When he spoke, his voice was soft. "You look lost," the man said. He had a nice smile. "Are you waiting for someone?" When I said no, he asked if I needed a place to sleep. I told him I'd reserved a room at Sloane House. His smile faded momentarily, but then he said that he knew Sloane House well. It was where he had stayed when he first came to New York. His name was Ted, he said, and he shared an apartment with roommates at Forty-third and Eighth. "You'll have to come by for a visit sometime," Ted said, and then offered to accompany me to the Y so that I wouldn't get lost. I couldn't believe my luck in meeting this helpful stranger. Together, we left the station and walked out into a light rain.

The glistening streets were bustling with people. Cars whizzed by; drivers beeped their horns. All around there was noise and movement, yet I found myself strangely unafraid. For a boy who'd been too frightened to venture out to the mailbox at home, I was easily navigating the city . . . and in broad daylight. There was safety for me in the city's anonymity. I walked with a jaunty step.

At the Y, the man at the desk greeted Ted like an old friend. I signed in, got a key, and carried my suitcase to my room. The door opened onto a space hardly bigger than a closet. It held a small bed, dresser, mirror, and sink (which I soon learned not to use because it reeked of urine, a result of previous occupants' reluctance to visit the hall bathroom when nature called). The room was overheated, the windows painted shut. But I was not alarmed. I had a room, a friend, hope for a job.

Ted had invited me to join him at a nearby diner—his treat—to celebrate my first day in New York. I quickly returned to the lobby, where he was waiting. We had coffee and a toasted bagel spread with cream cheese, a treat so exotic to a small-town boy that it might as well have been pâté de foie gras. I told Ted that I planned to look for a job the following morning, but I made an appointment to meet him in the afternoon near the lockers at Grand Central so he could help me retrieve my trunk.

That night, I couldn't sleep. The voices had made themselves at home in my new surroundings and quickly busied themselves devising new ways for me to destroy myself: In the big city, jumping from a skyscraper quickly replaced hanging from a tall tree as the suicide method of choice. Attempting to impose order on the chaos of my disordered mind, I reviewed the next morning's tasks: waking, showering, dressing for job interviews. I would show everyone— my parents, the voices—that I *could* make something of my life.

Monday morning, with the subways and buses not running, I walked to the first of three employment agencies listed in the classifieds. The woman at the reception desk dismissed me quickly because, she told me, I needed a high school diploma. At the second agency, I added a year to my age and a diploma to my credentials. *Liar,* chided the voices. *Shame on you. Don't you know that lying is a sin?*

The lie worked. There was an opening for a copyboy at Fairchild Publications, said the woman who interviewed me. She would set up an appointment for later that week.

"Why can't I go today?" I asked.

"You'll have to walk down to Twelfth Street and Fifth Avenue," she said. "That's miles away."

"That's okay, I don't mind walking," I said.

At Fairchild, publishers of *Women's Wear Daily,* I was directed to the personnel office. I filled out an application, was interviewed by a friendly woman in a blue suit, and toured the maze of offices with another copyboy. People were talking on the phone, clacking away at their typewriters, taking a break for yet another cup of coffee. My job would be to route mail to staff mailboxes. I returned to personnel, where the nice woman said that she'd been impressed by my willingness to hike two miles downtown for an interview. She hired me for the princely sum of sixty-five dollars a week, starting the following morning.

I was elated and couldn't wait to share my good news with my new friend.

"You're late," Ted said when I met him at the lockers.

"I'm sorry," I said, "but wait till you hear why. I just walked up here from my new job!"

He looked at me long and silently. It seemed to me that he was not pleased. Eventually, he said, "Well, let's get your trunk back to the Y. Then you can join me for lunch." I was eager to return to the Y so I could update my residential tenant card to reflect my new employment status.

At the diner, we were joined in the booth by another man. "This is Nick, a friend from the neighborhood," Ted said.

Nick was younger than Ted—in his twenties, I guessed—but he looked worn out. His skin was swarthy, and there were dark circles under his eyes, which seemed lifeless. His hair was thick and matted. Nick held out his hand and smiled, revealing yellow teeth. There was a diseased smell to his breath.

"Sorry," I said to Ted, stammering an excuse. "I forgot that I have to go back to the agency and pay them their fee. Maybe we can get together another time." Hurriedly, I backed out of the diner. The story about going back to the agency was true, but the reason for my leaving was to quickly put distance between Nick and me. I sensed something ominous about the man. It would be a while before I found out just how right I was.

My first few months in New York went reasonably well. Once or twice, I visited the Showcase Theater—the alleged reason for my coming to the city—but soon discovered that the writing program was a scam. I was given a few assignments having to do with the use of verbs—silly stuff that I was still sane enough to know not to pay for. Instead, I spent Saturdays at the main reading room of the New York Public Library. This incredible place would become my life raft time and again in the years ahead. For now, it offered a welcome alternative to my tiny room and, as always, a sanctuary from the voices.

My job offered no such respite. *Take a walk, Kenny. Find a good building to jump from. You've got the time. Let's see what buildings are available in the neighborhood.* As a copyboy, I could (and did) wander off for long periods without being missed. Sometimes, I would go to Schrafft's, a corner restaurant with marble floors, cloth-covered tables, a large counter, a case displaying chocolates for sale, and waitresses with crisp uniforms and starched white hats who created a wonderful feeling of calm and quiet. Every so often, I'd run into Ted there. He had some business in the area, he'd explain. Ted made a point of being available, and I generally was pleased to see him. For some reason, the voices never seized on Ted, never told me he was wicked or out to hurt me. I felt safe with him.

Ted and I might have a soda and sandwich at the counter. We'd talk for a while—about how the job was going, what I was planning to do that evening (stay in my room or go to the library on nights when it was open late). Eventually, I'd head back to the office, where I might drop off mail at the desks of publisher James Brady or film critic Rex Reed. Since the job demanded little interaction with other staff members, nobody commented on my long absences.

To my surprise, after a couple of months on the job, I was offered the position of editorial assistant at *Men's Wear* magazine, another Fairchild publication. This new job involved copywriting, for which I had some aptitude, and assisting the managing editor with mechanicals and layout, which was not my thing. But more to the point, it required that I be accountable and available. *They know you're a fake, Kenny,* jeered the voices. *You can't just sit here and look like you're busy. These people expect you to hand in something, something decent, and you're not going to be able to do it. You'd better disappear.*

And so I'd leave, letting my mind wander off into the world of the voices for several hours every day while my body remained at my desk. In my chaotic state, thoughts often came and went, and I could not catch them. Thoughts about dying and about how I would be mourned. Thoughts about destroying the voices. The work on my desk didn't engage me the way my favorite books had done. The next thing I knew, the managing editor was standing over me, saying, "Haven't you finished that job yet?" or, holding a set of galleys in his hand, "You clearly didn't proofread this thoroughly." I was making more and more errors. The editor warned me several times to shape up, but my mental turmoil prevented me from heeding those warnings. His was the outside world, and I was increasingly living in a world of inner demons. I found it impossible to concentrate on any one thing for more than a few minutes. My career as an editorial assistant turned out to be short-lived. I had lasted in the real world of work a little more than six months. I was laid off and given a generous four weeks' severance pay.

Losing the job meant losing whatever structure I had managed to impose on my life. And now I was also losing the salary on which I depended. Although I continued to receive a monthly allowance from my father, it wasn't enough to cover room and board. Nor did I feel that I could call home with news of my failure. I walked the city streets, alone with my voices, whose suicidal instructions were becoming increasingly persuasive. *Leap in front of a bus,* they said. In my delusionary state, I would step off the curb, but then the reality of being hit would return and, hastily, I'd jump back onto the sidewalk. "Watch out," people would yell. "Look where you're going, kid." I thought constantly about jumping from a building.

The fact that I'm here today is a sign of some greater power working in my life, I believe, since I'm now aware that one in thirteen schizophrenics do heed the instructions of their alien spirits to end their own lives. Many's the time that I came so close to being part of that awful statistic and stopped or was prevented by others from destroying myself.

One day toward the end of August 1966, when I was down to my last few dollars (and terrified that I would be evicted from my room for not paying the rent), I walked out on the street, where once again—by incredible chance, I thought—I happened to meet Ted outside the Y. "You look awful," he said. It may have been weeks since I had changed my clothes. My shirt was missing buttons; my pants hung on my slight frame. I didn't remember the last time I had eaten.

"I don't have money to do laundry," I said, as if that were the most troubling aspect of my situation. We went to lunch (Ted's treat again; I ate ravenously), then he gave me a handful of change for the washing machine. "Clean yourself up, kid," he said, "and I'll take you to dinner. Wear those jeans that I like—the white ones that are a little tight on you. And comb your hair."

I did as instructed, arriving at "our diner" at seven. By now, I knew many of the regulars by sight. They were not families having Sunday dinner after church. Ted signaled to me. He was with Nick, and somehow I was not surprised. Nor did I turn and run, as before. I moved heavily, as if sleep walking through a nightmare.

Ted greeted me. Nick nodded briefly, then got right to the point. "Do you owe Sloane House rent?"

"No, I'm paid up through tomorrow."

"Do you have any money?"

"No." I had spent all of my allowance. If I moved out of the Y without leaving a forwarding address and my dad sent me money, any mail directed to me would be marked RETURN TO SENDER. I realized that I had probably received my last check from home.

"Teddy found you, and he's taken a liking to you," Nick said. "Do you like him?"

"Yes, I do," I said truthfully.

"Ted wants you to have sex with him," said Nick. "Is that okay with you?"

To understand my answer, it's important to take you where I was at that time. Since I'd been fired, my fear of strangers had returned and, with it, my isolation. Once again, I had taken to spending entire days and nights in my room, the walls closing in on me, with no Grandma to bring me a hot supper and make sure I ate it. My sole companions were the voices, and they only reinforced my sense of defeat. In this state, the thought of *any* contact with a friendly human being seemed to offer some vague relief. As I saw it then, I had but two choices: phone my father and tell him I had failed or go with Ted. With great reluctance, I chose the latter.

I looked my friend Ted straight in the eyes. He was waiting for my answer. Turning away, I whispered, "Yes."

Nick then set forth the terms of my "employment."

"Understand, you work for me now," he said. "Teddy will give you a place to live, and he will feed and clothe you. Teddy gets you first because he recruited you. I'll have you when I'm in the mood. And then there are the customers— older men who like young boys. We call them chickenhawks. It's your job to keep them happy. I'll handle all appointments and financial arrangements. You bring any tips and gifts to me, and I'll give you some of what you bring in if I hear you're worth rewarding. Clear?"

I must have nodded, because Nick rose and walked out into the early night. Ted and I ate dinner in silence. Then we went to the Y, picked up my luggage, and took a cab to Ted's apartment, where we had sex. "You're one of the boys of Eighth Avenue now," Ted told me, his arms wrapped around me as he drifted off. But I did not sleep, and not just because my voices ranted at me without pause. *What would your priest think of you now? What would Grandma say if she could see her little Kenny? . . . So you came to the big city to be a tramp, a male queer whore. Well, aren't you proud that you've accomplished that! Dirty boy, you really deserve to die. Die, die, die.*

In a very real sense, a part of me had just done that.

And so I entered the world of the male hustler, a world that revolved around "dates," mostly meetings with middle-aged and older men at a hotel or apartment—all of them pre-arranged and prepaid. Less often, I would join other boys at one of the bars along Eighth Avenue where we were known and protected.

Eighth Avenue from Thirty-fourth to Forty-eighth Streets was dotted with triple XXX theaters that featured pornographic films or live sex acts and by bars that catered to either straight or gay clientele, all of whom were on the make. Nick owned several bars on the street. The ones his boys frequented, advertised in the gay press, were small, dimly lit places where "young entrepreneurs" would go to meet "older financiers." Those are actually the terms that were used. Against the wall were rows of round tables where we boys would be seated. Customers would sit at the bar, looking us over. (According to the rules of the game, we were prohibited from sitting at the bar unless invited by a customer.) Generally, customers would express interest in a particular young "entrepreneur" by sending over a drink, or they would approach the table to negotiate a price or a sexual practice. We would refer them to Nick or Ted, one of whom was always seated at the bar during the times we were there. A nod meant that we were to accept the offer. If the "financier" was unknown to them, they'd have us followed to our destination by someone from the organization, called the Man/Boy Call Service, to protect their inventory. Being a hustler has this in common with being a schizophrenic: The bizarre becomes normal. And I was both.

As a new acquisition, I was in great demand. Still, whenever my date was over, late night or early morning, I returned "home," where Ted was waiting. He expected our relationship to continue on a sex-on-demand basis, meaning every night, and was visibly upset when I told him, one night, that I couldn't do that and handle all the other men. It was part of our bargain, he said. He had made many sacrifices for me, he reminded me. He had clothed and fed me. Since meeting me, he had sent his other roommates away. All of that was true, but to my own amazement I stood my ground, and Ted reluctantly agreed to give me breathing room.

A few days later, he told me that Nick wanted to see me at his place. I was nervous as I headed for Greenwich Village late that afternoon. I thought Nick was going to tell me off but good for defying Ted, and I wasn't sure how I'd respond. By the time I reached the four-story brownstone where Nick lived, I was in a state of near panic.

My first impression of Nick's apartment was that it was elegant—high ceilings, brick walls, working fireplace—and that it was clean, a surprise given that its owner always looked as if he could use a good scrubbing. Nick was a night creature. If he hadn't existed in the real world, he's the kind of demon that my schizophrenic mind would have created. I stared at him now. He was not wearing a shirt, and I noticed that, like an animal, he had dark hair covering both chest and back. Feeling revulsion, I stepped back into the hallway.

"Come on in, Kenny."

I reentered, and Nick closed the door behind me.

"The time has come for me to have the boy they're all raving about," he said, pulling me toward him. He kissed me, putting his tongue in my mouth. I gagged. I was prey in the hands of the predator.

"Be vigilant; because your adversary the devil, as a roaring lion, walketh about, seeking whom he may devour." In that instant, I heard Grandma's voice and grasped the true meaning of the Scripture she had quoted me in what now seemed a lifetime ago. For surely, Nick was the devil. It followed, then, that letting him devour me would be an unpardonable sin.

I thought, *I'd rather go out and kill myself than do this.*

I told Nick I had to wash up and would join him afterward. As he went into the bedroom, I made for the front door, opened it, and bolted down the stairs and into the street. I ran like a marathoner, pausing only to catch my breath. All night long, I alternately ran and staggered, not knowing where I was headed or what I was going to do. I stopped and stared into restaurants, looking at the food and the people inside. I did not sleep or eat. Sometime the next day, I found my way to the entrance of the main library at Fifth Avenue and Fortieth Street. I went inside. My feet ached. My shoes—the same ones I had worn when I left home—had holes in the soles. I remember wishing I could take off the shoes and soothe my feet against the cool marble floors. Among the stacks, I found a book about World War II and took it to a table in the wood-paneled main reading room, where I alternately read and dozed until a guard gently nudged me and told me the library was closing.

Back outside the entrance, I was startled by the pair of large marble lions that stand guard before the building. *"Your adversary, as a roaring lion, walketh about . . . "* Superimposed on the lion's visage I saw Nick's face surrounded by a mane of matted hair. The sight of the library lions usually comforted me, but in my frenzied state I feared the wrath of the Nick-lions. I was convinced that Nick and Ted were out hunting for me and that, if they caught me, I'd be forced to do the unthinkable. I saw Nick's face on every person who passed, and I trembled with terror.

My only way out was to heed the voices. Walking the streets in the darkening city, I searched for a building to jump from. *This is the time to find the building . . . the building that touches the sky . . . and you can jump. That's the way to do it, Kenny, jump and die.* Buildings with fire escapes wouldn't do. I could easily climb up, I reasoned (as if reason had anything to do with it!), but they were only six stories high, and I had to be sure that I'd be dead, not maimed.

"What business do you have here? Who are you going to see?" When I couldn't come up with an answer, I was turned away by the security guard at the Empire State Building. Disheveled and muttering to myself, I didn't look like the kind of person you want roaming around any place you're guarding. Other buildings, other doormen . . . again and again, I was stopped and turned away. Heading west, I managed to gain entry to several buildings that were unsecured and unguarded, but when I reached the top floor, I found access to the roof barred.

Finally, my search led to a building where, after walking countless steps from the ground floor to the top, I located a door that swung open to the roof. I had made it! Edging to the building's western perimeter, I looked down on a huge parking lot filled with postal trucks. Beyond the lot was an elevated highway where cars sped past one another in opposing directions, their headlights forming patterns of ribbons on the roadway. The scene was dizzying. I lowered myself to the tar surface of the roof, crawled to a space at the corner where I would be sheltered on two sides, and slept till dawn.

The hours that followed are hazy in my memory. I must have paced the roof. I know that at some point I sat on the edge of the building, my feet dangling over the side, and looked down, trying to decide the best spot to hit the ground. As I was plotting my death, I was unaware that the buildings around me, buildings even taller than the one I had found, were coming to life. People were turning on lights, getting cups of coffee, going to their desks, looking out the window.

I can only imagine the horror they felt when they saw me perched precariously at the building's rim, how they called to one another to verify what they were seeing, and how they then phoned for help. "Hurry! It's an emergency! There's a guy on the roof of the building across the way, and he looks like he's going to jump!"

Suddenly, the roof filled with a large cast of characters—police, firefighters, ambulance workers, voices—all bent on assaulting me. *Look at all the people,* my voices were saying. *They're here to push you over if you don't do it yourself. Coward. Do it now.* At the same time, the police officers attacked me with *their* questions: "How did you get up here? Did somebody let you in? How long have you been here? *Why* are you here?"

Bombarded by sound and confusion, I stood like a deer caught in headlights, unable to move or make a sound.

"Stop yelling at him and he may answer you." The speaker, a man in a regular business suit, took command. The outside voices quieted down.

"Why are you here, son?" the speaker asked me in a normal, conversational voice.

"I'm here because I want to die."

"Why do you want to die?"

"I'm being commanded to jump off this building."

"By whom?"

"The voices are telling me to do it. They're telling me not to wait. If I don't do it myself, they will follow me to hell. I have to do it myself. I have to do it now." I crept closer to the roof's edge.

"Get him!" shouted one of the police officers.

"Stand still," said the man in the suit firmly. I didn't know if he was speaking to me or to the officer. We both stopped.

"Go away," I said, pleading with everyone. "I don't want your help."

"Would you like the voices to stop without your having to die?" asked the man in the suit.

The circle of men seemed to be getting closer and closer to me. The voices were telling me, *See how they're drawing nearer? Be careful, Kenny. They're going to push you over. They're going to do your job for you. Do it yourself, do it now.* Perception or reality? In my mind's eye, I saw the circle closing in, and I drew back again.

"Wait," said the speaker. "I can help you. There is medicine that can make the voices go away. Would you like that? Come with me. Let's leave the building together, just the two of us. Let's go get rid of the voices." Slowly, he began walking toward me.

I let him take my hand and lead me to the door, not because of the promise of relief from the voices, but because I felt too confused and too worn out to make decisions. This is a common feeling in schizophrenia, one that I would experience many more times over the years. There was nothing else I could have done. It was December 1966—more than four years since the voices first spoke to me from my bedroom radio. In those years, they had taken me to New York; they had led me into a world of prostitution with its own rules and contorted images; they had urged me to climb to the top of this building and perch on the very edge of self-destruction. I went because I didn't know what else to do. And because a man who spoke gently was offering me direction.

An ambulance waited for me downstairs. Inside, I was placed in restraints and tied to a gurney so that I was unable to move, much less escape. With a police car leading the way, its siren blaring, I was taken to the emergency room of a city hospital—it must have been Bellevue—and shot in my buttocks with Thorazine, an antipsychotic drug that works as a sedative and tranquilizer. I felt wobbly. The dosage was so high, I couldn't stand or speak. It was like being a living potted plant, one that wants to spread and grow but is kept in its place by careful pruning. I think I was given a shot every four hours. My lips became very thick, as if they were growing a second or third layer of skin. They were dry and started to crack.

All of this did not happen in a day, of course. I lost track of just how long I remained in this hospital. I lost track of everything. For a time, I even lost track of the voices. They were as sedated as I.

And then they came back with a vengeance.

{ 4 }

Welcome to Bedlam

IFFERENT VOICES . . . People are speaking, I know, but I
can't decode what they're saying. Sounds of shuffling
feet . . . There's the feel of rough, callused hands against my
skin. Strong arms lift my own leaden arms, remove my shirt,
which is soaked as if I'd just come in from a downpour. My
pants, which also damply cling to me, are being pulled from
my body. The stench of urine is strong. The world is dark.

I am *rigid* with fear. This must be the hell that my voices
had threatened. That's it: I've died and God has sent me to hell.

My mouth is dry as the desert sand. Running my tongue
over cracked lips, I feel such sharp, intense pain that I'm sure
what is happening to me *must* be real. Where am I? Struggling to see my surroundings, I find my eyelids weighted
down. I panic. Have the voices blinded me now?

"Please, someone, anyone, help me. I've gone blind," I
shout. My voice is so hoarse, sound emerges as a whimper.

Come help him. Please come help him. Kenny's gone blind. Help! Help! He's blind! Poor, poor Kenny. My voices are back! *They think they can get rid of* us *by poisoning you, Kenny. They're fools. We're too strong for them to control. Strong enough to help you kill yourself. . . . Don't worry, when the time comes for you to die, we'll be around to tell you how to do it. . . . We understand what you want, Kenny. You'd rather be dead than be here.* The voices do not tell me where "here" is.

Thus begins my stay in Manhattan State Hospital on Wards Island, a 255-acre stretch of land in New York's East River that has housed the neediest cases in Manhattan—people whom no one knows what to do with—since Civil War days, when the Department of Charity and Corrections opened a "lunacy asylum" on the grounds. Manhattan State (currently known as Manhattan Psychiatric Center) was erected on the island in 1954. In 1967, I am taken from Bellevue and involuntarily admitted to Dunlap, one of three buildings that comprise the hospital complex (the others are Meyer and Kirby, all named for psychiatrists), and assigned to the "bad boys unit," a holding pen for adolescent and young adult males deemed dangerous to others or to themselves. Here I am tagged a "suicide watch" and placed in seclusion—a space not much larger than the narrow bathroom of my current apartment—where I am held under lock and key.

One "benefit" of the drugs and tranquilizers prescribed to treat my psychotic state is that they succeed in making me barely aware of my surroundings. Though I have no idea where I am, what I do know is that I am cold, that I am painfully constipated, that I feel like vomiting, that I am unable to see. I try moving my right hand toward my face to unglue my eyelids, but my arms are held fast against my body. Somehow, I believe, the voices have managed to tie me up. Powerless, I lie curled in a fetal position on a thin, plastic-covered mattress. There is no pillow. Mostly, I sleep.

Sounds of a key entering a lock and turning it, of a heavy door being opened. Someone is in the room.

"Who are you?" I call into the darkness.

A deep male voice, in an accent I identify as Jamaican, says, "C'mon and help me."

He is speaking to someone else, not to me. He and his helper take off my clothes with professional speed—a relief, since I had soiled them—and I say, "Thank you so much."

No one says, "You're welcome."

I try again. "My name is Ken. Can you tell me where I am?"

Sounds of movement. Suddenly, I am jolted by water so cold and forceful, it had to have come from a hose. The water has a strong smell of detergent. My eyelids, burning, remain closed. Next I am dressed in dry garments (a relief), but my pleasure is short-lived, for I'm quickly immobilized in a straitjacket. I don't have the strength to resist, let alone struggle to my feet. I return to the sleep of the drugged.

Awakened again by the sound of a key in the door, I hear a woman's voice this time. "He looks pretty helpless," she tells someone, adding, "Leave the door open while I feed him. I'll give a yell if he gives me any trouble." I recognize her accent as Latino. Something is pressed against my closed lips. "Open, man, it's food," says the woman. She feeds me. My tongue is thick. My parched throat hurts when I try to swallow. Unprepared for the container that is next offered me, I pull away, spilling much of its contents.

"Spill that milk, I won't get you any more," says the woman.

In desperate need of something cool and wet to drink, I say, "Please, I can't see. I couldn't see the cup."

"One half-pint of milk per patient per meal," she says. "That's the rule. No 'please' or 'thank you' is going to work on this girl, understand?" She doesn't offer me a second half-pint, but she gives me something more important. She replies to me—the first person in this place to do so.

"Yes, thank you," I say.

I hear her close and lock the door.

Comings and goings, always precipitated by the sound of a key in the door . . . Followed by voices:

"He's the jumper they committed here for observation?" asks someone in a low, female voice that sounds Indian. "Increase the meds by one hundred milligrams," she says.

"At every injection?" asks a man's voice.

"Four times a day by injection," answers the woman. "I'll sign the order."

"Please speak to me," I say to the two voices. "I think I've gone blind."

Without a word, the two people quickly move on and I am alone again, living in anticipation of hearing the next turn of a key in the lock.

During the more than two months that I remain in seclusion, my heart literally leaps at that sound. It is my lifeline— my only contact with voices other than the ones living in my head. I soon learn that the Jamaican man is named Devon, the Latina woman is Rosa, and there are also Miguel, Jose, Roberto, Lucinda, Myrtle, and Hyacinthe. If I am good— meaning if I am quiet—these outside voices might stay a while, talking to one another about their families, friends, joys and troubles. Their stories are like serialized books, and

I eagerly await each new installment. On the rare occasions when I speak up, the aides complete their business quickly and move on. Remaining silent, I might even be given a second container of milk or a pastry with some jam on it. I am learning the rules of this strange new world.

One day, the door opens and I feel myself being lifted into a chair and wheeled out of my cell. In the area to which I'm taken, someone washes me down quickly, then places a metal object in my hand and instructs, "Shave yourself."

I hold the shaver in a shaking hand, then say tremulously, "Sorry, I can't see to shave."

"What's all this about you can't see!" The speaker, whose voice I now recognize as belonging to Devon, places one strong hand at the back of my head, supporting me, while with the other he rips my eyelids apart. Light stabs at me, and I duck my head to avoid the pain. I blink, look toward the speaker, and see a light-skinned black man, muscular, about six feet four. "Let it go," he says, taking the razor from me. Then, to his fellow attendant: "He has no beard at all. But we have to get him cleaned up for the judge and the doctors. This man hasn't been in here for a washing since they admitted him over a month ago."

So I've been "here" more than a month! "What is this place?" I ask, hoping for an answer. "*Where* have I been all this time?"

"Listen to the man," says Devon. "He don't even know he's in Manhattan State."

Devon wheeled me into an amphitheater and positioned my chair in the center, facing a long table at which sat a half dozen white-coated men, whom I presumed were doctors, plus a judge from the New York State Department of Mental Hygiene. Two rows of darkened bleachers appeared to be filled with observers.

"You're very late," scolded one of the doctors at the table. I kept still.

"My apologies, Doctors," said Devon. "Steele was very difficult to transport. He made quite a fuss."

I hadn't, but I didn't contradict the man—and I was also grateful to him, for hadn't he opened my eyes? (I now understand that my "blindness" resulted from my being given too high a dose of Thorazine, causing contraction of my eyelid muscles, after which my eyelids remained shut, glued by a protein secretion. Try telling that to an eighteen-year-old who can't see and whose delusional voices explain everything as the work of evil forces.)

The doctors shuffled their papers, speaking to one another in muted tones, while twenty or thirty of *my* voices came at me from all directions.

You will die. . . . We will soon see the end of you. . . .

Get ready, Kenny. . . . You are *blind if you see safety in this place. . . .*

Why do you keep hanging around, Kenny? Didn't we show you how to die in the forest? Didn't we take you to the top of a tall building?

Why *didn't you jump?*

You failed. . . . We'll make sure you don't fail again.

The voices spoke not as a chorus, but one following the other, as if I had personally done each of them serious harm and it was time for retribution. Then, in one moment, they all went silent and only one voice—that of The Ruler—took over. *Your death is soon to come,* The Ruler prophesied. *Look over at that large clock.* A round white clock, circled in black, hung on the wall. *Notice the small hand slowly moving toward twelve o'clock. And whose head is at the number 12? Kenny Steele's head, of course. You have been very bad, Kenny. You have made much trouble for me and my band. Will our court decide to have your head cut off, or shall we have you be your own executioner?*

"Mr. Steele, do you know why you are here?" The speaker, a white-haired man seated at the table, was talking to me. I was startled. If I'd come to know anything about this place, it was that direct communication between staff and inmates was not permitted. So this had to be a trap! But I could avoid falling into it if I held my tongue. . . .

"Steele, I will ask you one more time. Why did you go up on that roof?" I did not answer. Nor did I respond to other questions: "Do you know what day it is? What month? What year?" (Truly, I did not.) "Do you hear voices? What are the voices telling you to do? Are you hearing voices now?"

I was, but I wouldn't tell the doctors. *Ticktock, ticktock, Kenny dies at twelve o'clock.* I looked up at the clock. The little hand was moving closer to twelve.

Then one of the doctors said, "Do you have any relatives other than your immediate family whom we can call? We've contacted your parents, and they've told us that, as far as they're concerned, you're eighteen and on your own."

My heart fell. I had been divorced by my parents! Since no one on earth cared about me anymore, I reasoned that I had nothing to lose by giving in. I began to speak, but the words tumbled out one over the other, garbled, incomprehensible. What was happening to me? Were the voices responsible for my tongue being so swollen, making my speech slurred and thick? I had so much to say, I struggled to get out one coherent thought: *Please help me. I don't understand what is happening to me.* But the doctors heard gibberish.

Through corridors painted a sickly yellow-green, Devon wheeled me back to my room. Once inside, he helped me from the chair and—more gently than before, it seemed— lowered me to my mattress. Devon left without a word. Alone, I began to relive the events that had just taken place: what the doctors had said, what I had *not* said. I was filled with rage because I guessed that I was doomed to remain here until the next hearing, whenever that would be. The panic was back—accompanied, as usual, by the voices and their incessant commands.

What a loser! You know your life is over, they told me. *Unless you kill yourself, you will live like this—an animal—for the rest of your life, with us as the only people who talk to you. . . . You have to kill yourself, Kenny. There is no other way.*

"Okay," I told my voices in a whisper. "You win. Just get me out of here and I will do your bidding. I promise I will kill myself." I meant to keep that promise. But first, I had to get out.

With my sight restored, I found a way to track time's passage by marking the late-afternoon light that shone through the large keyhole in my door. (My dinner would arrive soon afterward.) In this way, I counted the days from sunset to sunset. After twenty-six sunsets, my door was swung open. Once again, Devon and one of his helpers assisted me into the wheelchair. This time, they didn't race along the yellow-green halls. They also took their time in washing me down. They cut my hair short. They made me presentable. Then they wheeled me into the amphitheater, where once again my tribunal waited.

Now I answered the questions put to me to the best of my ability. I looked up at the big white timepiece on the wall. It was just a clock. To my surprise, my voices did not intrude on this hearing. At its conclusion, the judge said, "You understand, Mr. Steele, we are giving you dayroom privileges based on your good appearance and orderly conduct today as well as good reports from the staff. We'll start with four hours a day and expand that if you pose no problems. You have, however, been committed to us for an indefinite period, so I suggest that you work very hard at doing what you are told."

I tried to sort out the messages I'd just heard: One, I was here for an indefinite period. Two, I would get to spend at least four hours a day out of seclusion.

"Thank you," I said.

Devon wheeled me back to my room, and then he did an incredible thing—he spoke to me. "You did real good, man. Real good." He and Jose helped me out of the straitjacket and into bedclothes. "They took the jacket off because you've been good," Devon said. "Don't make no trouble or you'll be back in it again." I smiled at Devon and Jose. They smiled back, then went out and locked the door behind them.

Only those who have been physically restrained for long periods can know the mixed feelings of relief and pain that accompany release. There's a saying that a man must learn to crawl before he can walk and walk before he can run. Stubbornly, I strove to be able to stand, next to move about my small world, and finally to exercise, which I needed to do in order to regain my strength. Exercising was often agonizing, but it was even more painful not to do so. This habit followed me through years of hospitalizations, times when I would be separated from other patients and placed in rooms described by a variety of names: separation, solitude, retreat, quiet, and privacy. (Patients had other names for these places, among them: solitary, torture chamber, the hole. Many, though not all, of the rooms *were* used as a form of punishment, and patients' names for them reflected this mistreatment.)

I did push-ups and sit-ups. I paced the rectangle of my room. When I was ten years old, I'd gone on vacation with my family to Washington, D.C. Now I pretended to be climbing the stairs of the Washington Monument, all 897 of them. When not working out, I sat on my mattress and rocked back and forth, back and forth. It wasn't a planned part of my exercise regimen.

"Six o'clock showers!" The morning call, from outside my room, had me up and hopeful. My door was unlocked, and two attendants waved me forward. They flanked me on either side as I walked slowly to the showers, noticing—for the first time—other patients and attendants. I was led to an area with three private shower stalls and directed to use one of them. It felt wonderful to soap myself down, wash my hair by myself, dry myself off. . . . *My self.* Each detail of my grooming—liquid soap, mentholated toothpaste, mint-flavored mouthwash—was a gift, a recognition that I was a human being. I was handed clean clothes—underwear, pajamas, bathrobe, socks, green foam slippers that were too small for my feet—which I put on quickly. The attendants then led me to a different chair, one with a tray that they locked in place as a restraint, and wheeled me back into the hallway.

A few patients, many of them dressed in pajamas as I was, shuffled by. A tough-looking fellow, whom I guessed to be in his late twenties, glared at me. I met his fierce gaze. All of a sudden, a window was opened in what had appeared to be a windowless corridor. A man stuck his head out of the booth and called out, "Medications!" The fellow who'd been staring at me moved forward.

"You're not first today, Arnie," the man in the booth told him. Then he called to my attendants, "Bring Steele up here so I can get his meds out of the way."

As I was being wheeled forward, Arnie approached. Shoving his face right up to mine, he opened his mouth to reveal two large canine teeth. "Vampire teeth to suck the blood of young boys like you," he growled at me. My insides were quaking, but I managed not to flinch and returned his stare with one that I hoped was equally menacing. My brief life as one of the boys of Eighth Avenue had taught me some survival tricks. I couldn't let him know how frightened I felt or I'd be easy prey.

"So you're our latest flyer," said the man who dispensed the medication. "We haven't had one in a while. I'm Mr. Brown, the nurse here. You'll need to drink this medication in front of me. I have to make sure you swallow it. It's the same stuff you've been receiving, but in liquid form. I imagine you'd prefer to get it this way. Your butt must hurt something awful from all those shots." I nodded. "Now you behave on my shift, boy, and we'll get off to a good start. Okay?" Again I nodded. I wasn't looking for trouble.

"We're taking you into the dayroom now," one of my two attendants said after I'd swallowed the medication. Every transition was fraught with terror for me. "One or both of us will be an arm's length away at all times," he said. "If you need to go to the bathroom, just signal us. Ignore any patients who want to get into it with you, and cause no problems."

Sunlight streamed into the dayroom through a wall of high windows. A couple of people were already there. Soon others wandered in. Dark-skinned male attendants in white uniforms. Patients dressed in pajamas and robes or rumpled khaki outfits. (Later, I, too, was given such a uniform: khaki pants and shirts, clean underwear, socks, regular shoes—everything bore the label MANHATTAN STATE HOSPITAL.)

My reputation had preceded my appearance. The unit's residents knew I had been held in seclusion for two months. The reason, they'd been told, was that I was a madman, someone who shouldn't be messed with, for I was capable of exploding. (Devon had started that rumor, I later discovered. He wanted to protect me.)

I was convinced that every person in the room was staring at me, and I almost longed for the safety of seclusion. A characteristic of schizophrenia is that it typically leads people to be very grandiose. In my delusional state, I was the central person in every drama, and I believed that everything that happened took place because of me. If people were ill, it was because of me; if well, because of me. I was paranoid to the point that when a space shuttle exploded, I *knew* that it was because of me—I had some psychic power to make that happen. That's what my voices told me, replaying every event. *It's your fault, Kenny,* they'd say. *For the sake of the world, you must be destroyed.*

With a good deal of hesitation, I surveyed my present world. Some of the patients in the dayroom were about my age. Others appeared to be in their twenties; Arnie looked the oldest. Mostly, they paced about in circles. Some talked to themselves. One fellow approached and told me he was Jesus Christ. (He was the first Jesus of many I would encounter during my years in mental institutions.) "Back off," said one of my attendants, shooing the savior away.

There were about forty-five patients and some thirty chairs. (In the days and weeks that followed, I discovered that the same people occupied the same seats every day and that the chairs seemed to be bolted down. They remained in one spot. This was important because at least two or three fights would break out each day and they were often because someone invaded "home base," meaning that he sat on another person's chair.) The sitters rocked back and forth in a motion I quickly recognized as my own, concluding that it must be characteristic of my illness, schizophrenia, and that they had to be fellow sufferers. I did not know that, like me, the residents of the unit were all medicated, and the constant pacing and rocking—that desire to keep moving— was akathisia, a common side effect of the antipsychotic medicines.

"Breakfast will be here soon," a boy with a crew cut whispered, sidling past my chair. *That one's a killer,* warned my voices about the boy. *And the one over there—leaning against the window—he'll suck the blood from you.* They were talking about Arnie, who soon left his position at the window and approached my chair. "Just wait till you're in the dorms," he said threateningly.

"Leave him alone," said the boy with the crew cut.

In a flash, Arnie turned and started viciously pummeling him, setting off screams and cries among some of the patients while others continued their pacing and muttering. Four attendants rushed the two fighters, pulled Arnie off the crew-cut boy, and dragged both men from the room. I sat frozen, fearful that I would be punished. I didn't have to be told that the fight took place because of me.

Welcome to Bedlam! shouted my voices.

I signaled Jose, one of my attendants.

"What's the matter, Steele?" he asked.

"Can I get a book?" I was desperate to find respite from the chaos and thought of the one thing that had worked for me in the past.

"All we've got right now are some magazines," said Jose, wheeling me across the room to an alcove that held a bookcase containing a dozen old copies of *Reader's Digest*. "I'll get you a book from the library some other time." I chose two magazines and found that I could still lose myself in a story. As I read about how a family survived a hurricane that destroyed their home and farm, I felt that I, too, might make it through my personal storm.

In this way, I managed to behave myself, and I was eventually allowed to spend all day—from six in the morning until six at night—in the dayroom. I was freed from my chair and permitted to move about. One day, I spied a vacant seat and approached it with caution. I knew it "belonged" to a wiry, agitated guy on the ward who frequently stared at me in a way that the voices warned was dangerous. *Watch out for that one, Kenny. He can kill.* Still, I wanted to rest, and so I warily sat down with a copy of *Reader's Digest* that I practically knew by heart. The chair's evil owner entered, and I quickly jumped up. "It's okay," he said good-naturedly—his voice was soft—and walked off toward the window.

Another pleasant surprise: That same day, Jose came over and handed me a copy of *Catcher in the Rye,* one of two favorite books I'd earlier requested. (The other was *Moby Dick.*) As I began to read, I was back in my bed at home where, as a junior high student, I had first encountered the tale of Holden Caulfield, Salinger's classic story about a teenager who drops out of prep school and spends the ensuing years hunting for identity and purpose in life. I felt Grandma's hand on my shoulder.

In fact, it was the hand of the doctor—a woman from either India or Pakistan, in her forties, with long black hair that she wore in a braid. "Mr. Steele, you no longer need your attendants," she said. "We've taken you off suicide watch." That was that.

As the doctor moved off, I noted that others in the room made a path for her, bowing and scraping as people do when they curry favor. Their appearance—straightened postures, hair newly slicked down—said, "Look at me," "Notice me." The staff later explained that she was the one psychiatrist for hundreds like me, a woman with the power to decide which of us crazy men would be granted privileges, which would be restrained.

Shortly after the doctor left, Mr. Brown, the nurse, approached and told me that she'd ordered a new medication for me. "You'll like this pill," he said. "It will combat the feeling you've complained about, of jumping out of your skin." Forty-five minutes after taking the pill, I could no longer focus on the words in my book. I told one of the attendants that I was having trouble reading, and he said he'd report it.

Mr. Brown's shift was over, but the attendant walked with me to the nurse on the second shift, a woman I'd not seen before, and told her of my situation. "It may be a side effect of your new medication, Cogentin," she said. "It often causes blurred vision. Don't worry. It's nothing serious."

Nothing serious? If I couldn't read, I wouldn't survive in this madhouse. My anger must have shown because just then another patient, a fellow with black hair and startling blue eyes who looked to be in his mid-twenties, put his fingers to his lips and, with his other hand, motioned me forward. I decided to risk it and edged toward him. "If you don't want to take the pill, tongue it," he whispered, demonstrating how he managed to hide his pill. "The important thing is not to make a fuss or they'll check up on you and force you to take it."

"Thanks," I said. "My name's Ken."

"I'm Anthony," he said. "I've been watching you, and I like to read, too. Would you do me a favor? For some reason, you've been able to get them to bring you books. I'm afraid to ask because they might say no. Would you get me a book?"

"What type of book?"

"You pick, but sports would be great," he said. Then he smiled and left, hugging the wall of the corridor on his way back to the bad boys' dayroom, where one patient would readily punch another's nose for a cigarette denied, a guy would leap at someone else for invading his territory, teeth would be knocked out and bones broken at slights both real and imagined. People were constantly being carted off to the medical unit. Another part of the daily routine was watching the big clock to see when breakfast, lunch, or dinner would be served, even though we knew full well that the food was inedible.

I continued to sleep in seclusion—a result of overcrowding in the wards rather than that I was still perceived as a danger to myself or to others. In 1967, there were 3,600 residents in Manhattan State. As many as fifty people would be housed on a ward that should have held no more than thirty-five. Patients were constantly yelling and screaming. I welcomed the chance to sleep alone. The door to my room was left unlocked.

One day, Mr. Brown told me I had a visitor. "Mr. Morris is here to see you," he said. I looked at him quizzically. "Mr. Morris," he repeated. "Ted Morris, your roommate. The social worker called him."

Ted was here! I didn't know how to react. "Is he alone?" I asked.

"Yes, but you don't have to see him if you don't want to. Almost everything we tell you in here is something you *have* to do, but we can't force you to see a visitor. It's your call."

"I'll see him," I said. Mr. Brown motioned to Roberto, an attendant, to join us. We walked down a long hallway, passed through two doors that needed to be unlocked to admit us, then locked behind us, and reached the visiting room.

"You have up to thirty minutes," Mr. Brown explained. "Roberto will be watching from right outside the room. Just let him know if you wish to leave before the time is up." He stopped and looked at me before unlocking the final door. "Understand?" I nodded.

The visiting room looked out at the Manhattan skyline. I felt as if I almost could touch the tall buildings, they were that near . . . and yet a world away from the life I was now leading. "It's a beautiful day out," said Ted, holding out his right hand. His left was circled around a cardboard cup that contained coffee.

I shook his hand. "How did you find out I was here?" I asked.

"Remember, you listed my name, address, and phone number on the identification card in your wallet where it asked for the person to be notified in case of emergency? Well, after you were brought in, a social worker called and asked about my connection to you. I told him we were room-mates. He asked if you'd be able to return to the apartment, and I said yes. I asked if I could visit, and he said not for a while but that he would call me as soon as you could see visitors. And he did."

I wondered how much Ted knew about what I had done. "Can you get me a cup of coffee?" I asked. "The stuff they give us here is dishwater."

"I can get you anything you want."

I asked the attendant if there was time for Ted to get me coffee. "No," he said. "But if he leaves you some money, I'll buy you a cup when I go on my break."

Ted handed me a twenty-dollar bill, plus several rolls of nickels and dimes. "You can use these to phone me at our apartment," he said. *Our apartment!* The words sounded strange in this place. Roberto took the money and wrote out a receipt. Ted was still talking. "I gave it to them," he said. "I hope that's all right."

"You gave what to whom?"

"When the social worker phoned me, I gave him your parents' number. You didn't have it in your wallet."

Your parents know about Ted, said my voices. *They know about you living with a man . . . and about all the other men.*

Your father was right. You're a sissy . . . a faggot . . . a whore. You can't go home again, even if you want to. This is your home now, Kenny. Do you like it?

My heart beat rapidly. Had the social worker phoned my parents and told them they could visit me? Were they staying away because they knew what I had been doing while living with Ted? "Ted, you have to help me get out," I said.

"We'll talk about it at my next visit," he said.

Our time was up. Ted handed me some candy bars that he'd brought with him. I gave him a hug, left the room, and walked back with the attendant.

"Anything you want to go with the coffee?" Roberto asked.

"Maybe . . . a sandwich? A submarine?" I asked hopefully.

"Sure," he said. "What kind?"

"You pick, and can I buy you something, too?"

"No thanks," he said. "You're a good guy, and I'm happy to do it. Just don't tell the others, okay? Then everyone will want favors."

"You have my word," I said.

Returning to the ward, I was the center of attention. "What did you get?" the inmates wanted to know. "Any money? Food? Cigarettes?" This ritual took place whenever someone had a visitor. No one was interested in *who* came to see you; the focus was on what they brought with them— and what the ward's bullies could manage to wrest from you.

"He didn't bring anything," I said, and quickly picked up my book, placing it before me as a shield. I was reading *Moby Dick* at the time. There were gripes and grumbles from some of the tough guys, but no one laid a hand on me. I think they saw me as a time bomb, innocent-enough looking but capable of a major explosion if set off.

Later that afternoon, Roberto made good on his promise, taking me aside and into a small room used by the staff. "It's lunchtime," he said. "Dig in." He had brought me a sub filled with lots of bologna and cheese, pickles and mayonnaise. I wolfed it down. It tasted better than any sirloin steak my dad had ever grilled.

That afternoon I also met Mr. O'Toole, who stood a couple of inches over me and had gray streaks in his brown hair, which was growing sparse. "I'm your social worker," he said, directing me to his office. He talked as we walked, asking me how my visit with Ted had gone and whether I planned to move back in with my roommate upon discharge. Once we were seated in his office, he said, "The staff feels that you no longer need to be on this ward and has recommended that you be moved to another unit where we can begin to plan for your discharge. How do you feel about that?"

I felt great. "How long would that take?" I asked.

"Well, first we need you to sign a form that will change your status from involuntary to voluntary admission," he said. He explained, "One reason we've been unable to move you to a more open ward environment has to do with the fact that you were committed involuntarily. Do you understand?"

I didn't really, but I nodded yes. I would have agreed to anything that would get me out of this place. "What else do I have to do?" I asked.

"Continue to behave well," he explained, "and be open to a transfer to another hospital."

"What other hospital?"

"Harlem Valley State Hospital," said Mr. O'Toole. "It's in a town called Wingdale. That's in Dutchess County, near Poughkeepsie, in New York."

Though I wished fervently to get off my unit, I was coming to know my way around Manhattan State and, strangely, felt some measure of safety here. The staff generally treated me well, and I'd even found one patient, Anthony, whom I could regard as a friend. "I don't want to leave New York City," I said.

The social worker was very patient with me. "Mr. Steele, if you want to get on to a voluntary status and to a rehabilitation ward where we can work toward discharge, Harlem Valley is the fastest way to go. We're overcrowded here, and there's a long wait for one of the rehabilitation wards." With that, he showed me a brochure about Harlem Valley, pointing out the grounds and some of the athletic facilities, like a travel agent trying to sell me on a vacation hotel.

He took out some papers requesting voluntary status for me to sign, and he informed me that once I became voluntary I would still have to give the authorities seventy-two hours' notice before leaving.

"Why?" I asked.

"It gives the doctors time to review your case and make sure you're not going to go out and try jumping from a building again," he said. My voluntary status would go into effect the following day, Friday, he explained, adding that it would be unwise for me to institute a request for discharge before a plan had been worked out at Harlem Valley. In the meantime, he continued, I would be granted ground privileges—the freedom to walk about on the hospital grounds without supervision.

When I returned to the ward, I shared this information with Anthony. "Have you ever had ground privileges?" I asked him.

"I have them now," he said.

I was surprised because I'd always seen him on the ward. "Why aren't you outside?" I asked.

"Because it's too easy to leave," he answered. "When I'm outside, I feel tempted to just get on the bus and go to my mom's house in the East Village. It's the same bus that the attendants use to get on and off the island. It goes into Manhattan. But you've got to make sure you don't leave right before or after shift-changing time, when the bus is full of people who work at the hospital. At other hours, there are just a few visitors. Whenever I escape," he added, "my mom calls the hospital and I'm back on a locked unit."

"But why back to the most violent ward?"

"Because sometimes I get real angry and I can't control myself," he explained. I had never seen that side of Anthony.

I asked if he would show me around the grounds, and he agreed. Then I phoned Ted and told him about leaving the island on the bus. He said it sounded like a good idea. My voices were all for it. *You have to leave at the first opportunity, Kenny,* they told me over and over again during the long weekend, which I spent restlessly, plotting my departure. *Then you can go back to the city, where there are a lot of big buildings. We'll find you a better building this time. We'll help you jump before they can get to you. You'll never come back here. You'll be dead like you promised. Remember?* I remembered.

Walking out of the tall brick building and into sunlight the following Monday morning was overwhelming. I'd never before thought about how much room God gives us and about how little we appreciate the gift. I marveled at the open space. Anthony showed me to a recreation facility, where we played a game of pool. He walked me over to the canteen. I treated the two of us to sandwiches and coffee with the money Ted had given me. We jogged a bit and talked. I looked at the cloudless expanse of sky and ached for my freedom.

Tuesday, Ted arrived for his visit. He carried one of my jackets that he thought I might like to wear outside. We had lunch at the canteen and then walked to the bus stop. I'd intended only to show him how an escape might be worked out, but when we reached the stop, few people were around. "Let's try it," he said quietly, and I obeyed, throwing the jacket over my clothes and ducking my head for fear of being recognized. I was scared down to my toes. As is typical for New Yorkers, no one looked up. Each rider sat alone in his world, and my big breakout went without incident as the driver took the turnoff at the Triborough Bridge and headed for 125th Street and Lexington Avenue. Once there, we took the crosstown bus over to the West Side, then the A train downtown, reaching Ted's place without incident.

"We're home," Ted said as we entered the apartment.

I knew what "home" meant, and soon I was back in bed with him. Afterward, I turned to Ted and told him, "No more prostitution for me."

Ted sat up and looked straight at me. "Nick won't buy that," he said. "Remember, he's pretty tough."

"Compared to the guys I just spent time with, Nick no longer scares me," I said.

"He should," said Ted, becoming very serious. "Nick has a way of getting even. Please don't take that attitude, Ken."

"Nick knows I'm here?"

"Of course," Ted said. "He expects you back. He's even got some dates lined up for you."

I got out of bed and threw a shirt on. *Faggot! Pig! Whore!* The voices were having a field day, and I found myself agreeing with them. I had to be the biggest fool in the world to put myself in this position again. I went to the kitchen, got myself a soda, then went into the living room to try to sort things out. My delusional voices were mixing with my own thoughts and Ted's admonition: "Don't try to mess with Nick, kid."

I didn't know what to do. I went back into the bedroom. "Is Nick coming over today?" I asked.

"Not till lunch tomorrow," Ted answered. "He promised that we could have twenty-four hours together before he'd start sending you out again. Come back to bed."

I spent the night wrestling Ted off me and trying to wrestle with what to do the next morning. I saw Nick's face, the face of a lion, and then I saw the faces of Devon, Anthony, and Mr. O'Toole, who had spoken of making real, solid discharge plans for me. Maybe I could get another job like the first one at Fairchild, where I didn't have to sit at a desk and be overwhelmed by my voices and delusions. Maybe, just maybe, I could make a life for myself.

I made up my mind to leave. In the early morning, I rose, washed, and dressed while Ted was still sleeping. Fortunately, I still had the twenty-dollar bill he had handed me at the start of our visit the day before. I let myself out of the apartment and flagged down a green-and-white taxi, asking the driver how much it would cost to get to Manhattan State Hospital on Wards Island. He didn't know where it was. The driver of the second taxi I hailed estimated the ride at about five dollars. (The fare was then thirty-five cents to start, plus five cents for every quarter mile.) I jumped in and headed back to a place that I'd thought was a living hell. *I guess I am a voluntary patient,* I thought. The voices scolded me. They made fun of me. They told me to jump out of the cab in Central Park, run to the lake, and drown myself. I fought against the urge to tell the driver to stop so that I could leap out and do their bidding.

When we got to the hospital, the meter read $4.80. "You were lucky," the driver said. "We didn't hit traffic at this hour."

"What time is it?" I asked.

"Six forty-five," he answered as I paid and got out of the cab.

I knew the canteen opened at seven, so I headed there, bought some coffee, then found a seat outside of Dunlap, hoping someone would come out and tell me what to do. The voices were so active, I no longer was able to think. *This is the last straw. . . . You actually brought us back here with you,* they said, one on top of another, as if I were in the subway during rush hour and loudspeakers were competing with the sounds of the surging throng. *You are a stupid, stupid kid. You think these people care more about you than your parents, who abandoned you here? Or your pimp? Or your boyfriend? A fine group of friends you have. We're your only friends, Kenny. It's about time you realized that and listened to us.*

After about an hour of waiting, I entered the building, climbed the many staircases to my ward, and rang the buzzer—as if only returning from ground privileges. Roberto opened the door. He said nothing but marched me straight to the nurses' station. I walked like an automaton.

Roberto noticed. "Are you hearing voices?" he asked.

I nodded without thinking. He took me into the same room I'd entered before being taken to seclusion. "Please don't lock me up!" I pleaded to no one in particular. "No big keys and door locks. Please! I left, but I came back on my own. I'm voluntary."

I heard Roberto tell someone I was hearing voices. His voice was like an overlay on top of theirs, as if they were outside me but he was in an altogether different room. That's how it always was in my delusional state. The voices surrounded me; others had to break through.

The Indian doctor entered, followed by another doctor and Mr. O'Toole, my social worker. Devon was there. "Steele doesn't require seclusion," I heard him say. "He did come back on his own. Maybe we gave him too much freedom too soon. Maybe we have to go slower. We can work with him on this ward. We know him."

"Sorry," Mr. O'Toole said. "The ward is too full. I can make arrangements for Harlem Valley to take him right away."

"Gentlemen," said the Indian doctor. "First, he's no longer here on a voluntary status. His escape changed all that."

"Please don't put me in seclusion," I said, interrupting her. I was that scared.

"Mr. Steele, did you think about jumping off a building or otherwise killing yourself while you were away?" she asked, looking directly at me.

I lowered my eyes. "My voices wanted me to kill myself," I said, "but I came back here for help."

I was trembling from inside out. The voices were angry that I had betrayed them. *We'll get you,* they said. *He is coming. You'd better prepare.* "He" must be the evil leader, The Ruler, I figured. The shaking grew worse. I felt myself drooling. . . .

When I came to, it was in another seclusion room. I was not wearing a straitjacket. I rose and walked to the door. My weight against it caused it to open. Roberto stood outside. "You passed out," he said. "They gave you a strong shot of Thorazine when you went in to see the doctor." I had no memory of receiving an injection, but I felt the sedation hangover that the medicine brought on—like my head was filled with cotton and I couldn't complete a thought.

"What happened? Am I locked in here?" I asked.

"Devon will tell you. I just sent him a message that you are awake."

It felt like I waited for hours (though it may have been ten minutes) for Devon to arrive. In the meantime, the voices painted a horrifying picture of my future. *You will be locked up for a long time,* they said. *Locked away with nothing to read, no one to talk to. You'll end up killing yourself, so do it now and save us all this trouble.*

"Kenny," said a male voice. It was the first time anyone—other than my voices—had used that name for me since I left home. Could it be my dad? My heart jumped. I looked up and it was Devon. I hadn't recognized his voice. "Please explain to me what happened out there. Your roommate says you followed him home and threatened him to allow you to stay. He says he phoned a friend, while you were sleeping, to help throw you out."

I could not tell Devon about my relationship with Ted. Gossip sped quickly through the ward. I didn't want him or anyone else to know about me. I looked Devon straight in the eyes. "I did nothing like that," I said. "I'm not lying to you. I promise. I went to where I used to live, stayed overnight, and when I woke I knew I was doing the wrong thing, running away, so I came back here. It's that simple."

"You surprised me by coming back," Devon said, and smiled. "It shows that you want to get well. I need to tell you the doctor's decision. Tomorrow morning you will be taken by van to Harlem Valley, where you will be placed in a ward like this one. Be good, and you can quickly become a voluntary patient again, with ground privileges. I'll get up there someday to see for myself that you're doing okay." (I found out later that Devon was a leader in the union for mental health attendants and knew staff members at other hospitals. In placing me under his care, God had been watching out for one of his sparrows.)

"Almost forgot," Devon said. "Anthony wanted you to know that he's agreed to go to Harlem Valley, too. It may be good for both of you to be where it isn't so crowded. Maybe you can get better care."

The two-hour drive to Wingdale, New York, the next morning took me through genteel villages reminiscent of the Connecticut valley landscape of my youth: green, rolling hills on which mostly modest houses were set, along with a few scattered mobile-home communities. Periodically, our van passed a farm and cows grazing or resting beneath a canopy of trees. As we turned off Route 22 onto the grounds of Harlem Valley State Hospital and I saw the ivy-covered buildings, I was reminded of the campus of Cheshire Academy for Boys, a prep school near my hometown. Everything outside the windows of the van spoke of tranquility, and I was lulled into believing I would be safe. I did not know I was about to enter the lions' den.

After completing the admissions process (lots of paperwork followed by meetings with a doctor and social worker), I was brought to my new ward. It was smaller than my unit at Dunlap. "Ah, the tough guy is here," said a familiar voice. I turned toward the speaker and met the gaze of Arnie, my nemesis at Manhattan State. "Better be careful, tough guy. I'm the main man here," he said. I was not unhappy when an attendant told me that I'd have to sleep in seclusion for the first week.

Dayroom life at Harlem Valley was much the same as at Manhattan State, except that the staff was less accommodating. No one brought me books here. And the atmosphere was more sexually charged. More than once I walked in on a scene in the showers and was surprised only by the time and place, not the act. Put young men together in a place without women, and sex between them happens. I had heard about such goings-on at night on Wards Island, but I'd never slept in the dormitories and so hadn't witnessed anything. No one had tried anything sexual with me. Still, there were fewer fights here than at Manhattan State, and even Arnie seemed to settle for a periodic growl in my direction. Toward the end of my first week, I phoned Anthony and told him, "It's okay here." He said that he would be transferred in two weeks and encouraged me to try to gain ground privileges before then. "Try to stay out of trouble," were his parting words.

Several nights later, trouble found me. Two men entered my room. I thought they were attendants, but I didn't recognize either one. In voices that were plainly disguised, they ordered me to get up. Once I was standing, they tied my hands behind my back and blindfolded me with a strip of the same coarse cloth, then led me to the showers. There they wet and soaped me down, holding me still as their hands and those of others explored my body. I screamed, "Stop it, please stop it," and they placed a gag in my mouth. I feared that I'd throw up and choke on my own vomit. Then they dragged me somewhere (back to my own seclusion room, I found out later), where one man after another mounted and raped me. Wave after wave of sharp, searing pain shot through my body. Nausea welled up in me as smells of blood and semen reached my open nostrils. My head was filled with the sounds of my voices, which came at me—as always—from outside my body.

Whore . . . sow . . . you're a piece of meat, they railed at me. *You're a ho now, any man's lay. Nobody decent will come near you now. We told you to die. You could have avoided this by hanging yourself. Finish it off, Kenny. End the story here.*

Then I heard the voice of The Ruler, loud and all too clear: *In nomine Patris, et Filii, et Spiritus sancti . . .* I felt—or believed I felt—the cross that my grandmother had given me being ripped from my neck. But I had not worn that cross in a long time. It had been taken from me when I first entered the mental hospital and was being held for safekeeping. Still, I felt the pull on the chain tugging my head backward. This image of the cross being ripped from my neck signaled the finality of anything good left inside me.

From outside the circle of my hallucinatory voices came the voices of the men who had just raped me. They were laughing. The voices sounded as if they came from another room, although the men surrounded me in my small cell. It's just that my delusional voices were closer, nearer to me, like a first circle of attack. "That'll teach you, Steele," called a voice from the outer circle.

I stopped struggling. It hurt less, I told myself. In fact, I no longer had the strength.

Then I lost consciousness.

{5}

Caught in the Revolving Door

I HEARD BUZZING, like the sound a fly makes hovering around an electric light. Looking up from my bed toward the ceiling, I saw a bright fluorescent light fixture and identified it as the source of the droning, which intensified the terrible ache in my head. The simple act of turning my face to the side set off a series of sharp pains that shot through me from head to toe. Tubes bandaged to my right hand climbed like ivy up a metal pole from which hung three bags filled with fluid.

I had been taken from Harlem Valley to a small hospital in a nearby Connecticut town, where I'd undergone surgery to repair the severing of the anal sphincter, a result of the rape. But what could be done to mend the sundering of my soul? A man entered and identified himself as my surgeon. "I know you're hurting," he said kindly. "See this gray button that I'm placing in your hand? I want you to push it when you need pain medication."

"Please don't make me ask for help, Doctor," I said. Harlem Valley had assigned attendants to watch me around the clock because I was still officially their responsibility: an involuntary admission who'd been placed on suicide watch. I gestured toward the pair, a man and a woman, who stood at the door. "I don't want the attendants to know anything about my pain," I said. I was concerned that they would go back to Harlem Valley and tell my tormentors that they had defeated me. I no longer trusted *anybody*.

The doctor seemed to understand. "Ring the buzzer three times and I'll let the nurses know that's your call for pain medication," he said, and left the room.

A television set was suspended from the ceiling to about two feet above the bed. One of the attendants turned it on, switching channels until she located her favorite soap opera. Once again, the TV became a conduit for my voices. *You have to get even, Kenny,* they sang in chorus. *You have to teach a lesson to those pigs who called you a ho. They fucked you. Now it's your turn. You have to fuck them back! . . . Kenny needs to hurt them* bad.

Never before had the voices instructed me to harm somebody else. But there was something different about me now. The voices zeroed in on the rage I was feeling. *We'll think up some great ideas for how you can get back at them, Kenny. . . . Leave it to us. We'll find a way for you to exact vengeance.*

I rang once for a nurse, who came quickly. "Please, can I speak to you in private?" I whispered.

She asked the attendants to step outside for a moment (they left grudgingly), then pulled the curtain around us. I told her I heard voices and that they grew louder and more intense whenever the television or radio was on. She immediately turned the TV off. "I'll leave orders to have it and the radio removed later today," she promised before returning to her station.

The attendants weren't happy with this. "Why'd you take our TV away, punk?" they complained. "Hell, we've got to spend eight hours each shift watching you lie in bed. You think you're that interesting, Steele? You think the world revolves around you now? Well, it don't."

My voices spoke for me. *Fuck you. We'll get back at you later, assholes.* I closed my eyes and lay still.

There was only one person I needed to speak to, and quickly. That was Anthony. At my request, a nurse brought in a telephone the following afternoon and placed a call to Manhattan State Hospital, where, by prearrangement, Anthony waited at the pay phone. "Don't come up to Harlem Valley under any circumstances," I warned him. "It's very dangerous and a hundred times worse than Manhattan State." I must have said *very dangerous* at least ten times during the three minutes we spoke. I didn't tell Anthony what had happened to me but felt grateful that, at the very least, I'd protected him from a similar assault.

My three-week stay in the hospital went by too quickly, for here people treated me kindly, bringing me medicine and books—both of which dulled the physical pain and mental anguish I continued to suffer. I wished I could have stayed on forever, but that wasn't possible. Instead, I was returned to Harlem Valley, continuing a schizophrenic odyssey that would find me cycling in and out of hospitals and halfway houses from Maine to Hawaii and points in between. Caught up in the revolving door of the mental health system, I'd go round and round, without really getting anywhere at all.

This time at Harlem Valley, I was assigned to the infirmary, a locked facility that mainly housed a geriatric population. I lay in a hospital-style bed, which was placed in the hallway where I could be observed by the staff. Several of the older residents thought I was their son or grandson. Two women said I was their father. Another believed I was her husband and scolded me for spending too little time with her.

For the most part, these old people sat in the dayroom and stared without looking at a television set that was kept on morning and night. I wondered if, like me, they heard voices coming from it. Once my health improved and I was able to get about, although with difficulty, I read to the old folks from a mystery novel I'd found on one of the tables. Some of the men and women were able to follow the story and looked forward to hearing the next chapter; others, less focused, simply enjoyed the attention of being read to. One April day, I happened upon a newspaper that must have been left on the unit by a staff member or visitor. It was about two weeks old. Martin Luther King had been murdered while I lay in the hospital! In some indefinable way, I knew I'd had a hand in his death.

Another sunny afternoon, a nurse approached me as I sat reading in my wheelchair. She asked if I wished to receive Communion. "No," I answered automatically. *No Communion for you, Kenny,* was the instruction I heard. Later, however, I noticed the priest on the ward. He was a sturdily built man, in his fifties I guessed, and he looked to be gentle. He seemed really to listen to the old people; he didn't just pat them on the shoulder before moving on. I wheeled my chair over to the nurses' station. "Can I speak with the father?" I asked the nurse on duty.

I don't recall what Father Luke and I talked about during that first visit and subsequent ones, but I came to look forward to our chats. Eventually, I grew comfortable enough to dare ask if he would hear my confession. He consented. As we sat together in a shaded vestibule off the dayroom, my life story tumbled out of me in a disjointed, epic confession. I told Father Luke about my voices and that I had been doing their will when I attempted the unforgivable act of suicide by trying to jump from a tall building. I confessed my feelings of hatred for the attendants at Harlem Valley and for any others whose heinous acts were responsible for sending me here. I spoke of how frightened I was of my new lust for vengeance. It brought dark clouds into my mind, clouds that remained even when the voices paused in spewing their venom. I confessed to the sin of prostitution. I even provided the father with details of the rape—something I had not been able to think about before, let alone put into words.

When it was over, I sat looking down at the floor.

The good father absolved me of my sins. "God has forgiven you," he said. "Now you must work on forgiving yourself." Leaving a prayer book with me, he asked me to read from it every day. My tears fell on its white leather covering.

At his next visit, Father Luke told me I would not be returning to my ward at Harlem Valley. I felt great relief at the news. And, he said, once I was well enough to leave the infirmary, I could be transferred back to Manhattan State if I wished. If I wished! We began the paperwork for my transfer immediately.

A month later, right about the time that Robert Kennedy was killed (my fault again), I was readmitted to the Dunlap building at Manhattan State, this time as a voluntary patient.

Following a brief stay on another locked admissions unit, I was transferred to an open ward and granted ground privileges. Outside one day, I ran into Anthony; ours was a joyful reunion.

It took a while for me to become a candidate for discharge. "It's important that you demonstrate a consistent pattern of good behavior and that the doctors are comfortable that your medication is working before we can consider it," explained my new social worker, Mr. Marks. The truth is, I was tonguing whatever pills were meted out to me. I couldn't take a chance on suffering the medicine's side effects: akathisia, blurry vision, stomach aches, nausea. I chose instead to deal with my voices, which had left off directing me to hurt others and returned to instructing me on ways to effect my own demise.

Life on the ward fell into a manageable routine. Mornings began with Community Meeting, where announcements were made about changes in privileges or discharge plans. Fridays, we'd find out whether our requests for a weekend pass were granted. Anthony and I had asked for a day pass, during the weekend, so we could go into the city and see the latest James Bond movie. Request denied.

Other ward activities included group therapy sessions (though therapy for whom, I could not tell you). The gatherings were typical of what passed for help at many state institutions for the mentally ill. Ten or twelve of us would sit around in a semicircle, facing a staff member who served as group leader. We patients were supposed to talk about things that were on our minds. One man insisted that he, not Lyndon Johnson, was the president and that he'd been locked away here by conspirators. Another talked about the relative merits of hanging versus poison as a means of suicide. We had two men claiming to be Moses—one bearded, the other clean shaven—a Jesus Christ or two, and celebrities enough to fill the pages of a glossy magazine. Often the group leader would single someone out and ask, laughing, "What's *your* line today?"

"And you, Steele?" she said, turning to me one morning. Her voice came at me from the outer rim, for I had not been taking my medication and was lost in the din of my hallucinatory voices.

I started, like a schoolboy caught not paying attention. "Ask me no questions, I'll tell you no lies," I replied. Without comment, she moved on to the next person in the circle.

Soon Anthony was discharged to the care of his family. "If you had a family that would take you back, your chances for discharge would be far better," Mr. Marks told me after Anthony and I had said good-bye. "But that's not possible," he went on, shrugging his shoulders. "Your parents have a young child and feel that they can't take any chances." He brightened. "They recently sent you some money, though— the rest of the insurance money, they said to tell you. You can put it in savings or use it to cover expenses here."

My body went numb. My father and mother had been in communication with people at the hospital, had told them about my baby brother, had even sent money, but they had never visited, had not even phoned me. If my parents had stayed by my side from early on, if they'd supported me, who knows what a different course my illness might have taken. I wish someone in authority had given them the advice I now offer to parents of young people with mental illness— parents who are concerned because their sons and daughters are isolating themselves, behaving erratically, not taking their medication, or are hospitalized. I tell them to continue to offer support, to let their children know they are there for them, but to take care of themselves as well. I also advise them (whenever possible) to share the care, to involve other family members in helping the sick person, so that they don't burn out.

Luckily, my friend Anthony had his parents. And I? I had a check.

I tried to maintain my composure in front of Mr. Marks, but my voices were having a field day with his news. *Told you this would happen, Kenny, didn't we?* they screamed at me. *The baby himself told you, way back when he was in your mother's stomach.*

"Look at me," Mr. Marks said as he gently put a hand to my chin and lifted it. My face was covered with tears. "This is progress," he said softly, handing me a tissue. "Anyone would cry given what I just told you. And then, with Anthony leaving, you must feel very sad. But look how well you are managing these events. This is what we mean by showing appropriate behavior and maintaining your impulse control. I am very encouraged by this." Because I characteristically showed little expression and the voices disordered my thoughts and feelings, Mr. Marks believed I was behaving well in appropriately expressing grief. I didn't tell him what the voices were saying . . . or that I hadn't taken my medication for a very long time.

I began to think more and more about suicide, even beyond the insistent commands of my voices. I wondered what kind of life lay before me. My one real friend was gone; I'd been disowned by my family; I'd cut off all ties with Ted. Perhaps I *would* be discharged someday—but to what? I had never felt this alone before.

The voices were all I had. They urged me to escape.

Take the bus . . . the same bus that carried you from the island the last time. You can go to New York, and from there you can find a forest. A forest of thick trees where you can hide. . . . We'll guide you, we'll guide you, we'll guide you the rest of the way.

At times, I saw the voices—or at least I think I saw them. Hallucination or imagination? I don't know, but the vision was real . . . and horrifying. The Ruler, whose identity had been provided by my grandmother, was the devil—not Satan with a red face and horns, but a larger-than-life wolf-creature that stood erect on two legs. The ubiquitous other voices, those lesser demons, were a pack of dogs, yet they were also human. Wolf, dogs, people—all came bearing down on me.

Acting on their instructions, I went to the administration building and withdrew twenty-five dollars from my account, leaving behind the balance of the money sent by my parents. I didn't want their money. Then I boarded a bus to Manhattan. Once there, I walked and walked aimlessly, grateful to find a park bench where I could rest every once in a while. Drawn to grass and trees, I walked toward Riverside Drive and the Henry Hudson Parkway, where I held out my thumb and caught a ride with a man who told me he was heading to Massachusetts. I said I was going that way, too.

Four hours later, he dropped me off somewhere in Boston. Again I walked, remembering places like the Old North Church and Paul Revere House that I'd read about in histories of the Revolutionary War. I spent two to three months wandering the Boston area, sleeping in doorways when I grew too tired or confused to go on. For a time, I set up house in one of the parks, making a bed out of leaves that I gathered and then covered with a plastic garbage bag to keep the mound safe and dry during the day. At night or when there was rain, the plastic served as either a tent or raincoat. There were public toilets nearby; one of them remained open at night.

In my wandering, I found my way to the South End and its several missions with soup kitchens, where volunteers generously ladled out meals to the hapless and homeless. The food was no worse, and sometimes better, than what I'd been served in state hospitals. I foraged through bins behind restaurants, grateful for scraps that others threw away.

Voices dogged my every step. *Look at you, Kenny. You're really a mess. . . . Look at your hair . . . it's matted, like a dog that's just come out of the water. . . . When was the last time you washed? You stink, Kenny. Phew. Nobody wants to get anywhere near you.* The voices were right. People made room for me when I passed by. Catching a glimpse of myself in a store mirror, I was shocked by my changed appearance. In my early twenties, I looked old and weathered. I *felt* old. My skin had turned dark and leathery, a result of constant exposure to the elements. My hair was long and unkempt. My clothing, soiled and rumpled, hung loose on my gaunt frame. If *I'd* seen me coming, I would have crossed the street.

I must have been acting strange, too, for I was picked up by the police one day and taken to Metropolitan State Hospital in Waltham, Massachusetts. The hospital, which closed in 1992, was made up of several brick buildings that housed about 500 patients. As usual, I was admitted as an involuntary placement. "Some people reported you," was all that the nurse on my ward would say.

"Take it," she commanded, handing me my medication. I did as I was told.

Haldol, the drug she'd ordered me to take, brought on the most frightening side effects I'd yet experienced. The symptoms were similar to those in Parkinson's disease. By blocking the nerves that control relatively gross motor movements, Haldol made me feel like the Tin Man from the *Wizard of Oz,* without any oiling. I moved stiffly and with extreme slowness. My jaw was rigid, and I actually was afraid that I would swallow my own, swollen tongue. No, not just afraid, but terrified. *They're strangling you,* said my voices gleefully. *Strangling you with your own tongue. That ought to put an end to this farce of a life.*

It seemed an eternity before a doctor came to see me. He gave me a shot (probably Cogentin), then casually poured himself a cup of coffee at the nurses' station and sat reading a paper while I stood transfixed, uncertain of what to do and sure that I was about to die. Eventually, someone helped me to a bed, where, in time, the stiffness and panic subsided.

Though I had no visitors, I was by no means alone. In the wards and hallways of the institution, I felt the presence of souls who preceded me here. The first of these ghosts to speak to me was a young woman. "You remind me of my Sean," I heard one day. The voice was soft and playful.

"Who are you?" I asked. I did not see her; I never saw any of the ghosts whose voices I heard.

"I'm Leslie," she said. "You have the same attitude as my Sean." I didn't understand what she meant by *attitude,* but from the way she said it, I sensed it was something positive.

Later, Sean approached and told me their story. "Leslie had just come from Europe with her family," he said. (That explained the hint of a foreign accent in her speech.) "She became ill, and her parents didn't know how to care for her. They put her in this hospital, where we met and fell in love." Sean and Leslie would frequently visit me during my two years at Metropolitan. Sometimes, Leslie would confide in me. Then Sean would get mad at her for telling me things he didn't want me to know. Theirs was an ongoing love story.

Another recurrent visitor was an old seafarer, a retired captain of a high-masted schooner, who had been in the slave trade when it was legal, had then gone loony, and had ended up in the hospital. The captain told me about sailing around the Horn of Africa, visiting Madagascar and other ports of call. His stories were those of adventure.

The voices of the storytellers were not threatening. They never ordered me to hurt myself, never yelled or screamed. Like the characters I met in books, they provided respite from the evil voices—perhaps because their narratives had nothing to do with me and I could lose myself in the imaginary worlds that they painted for me. Over the years, they would reappear in my life at different times and in various places. Unlike the evil voices, they were always welcome.

I gained ground privileges quickly and soon was assigned to an on-site workshop where I even earned a few dollars a week doing assembly-line work on industrial products— much as I might have done had I stayed at home and gone to work at Timex or another local factory. The monotony of the work suited me (perhaps it's in the genes, I thought), as did the fact that conversation with coworkers was not encouraged here. I wanted no more friendships so that I'd never again have to mourn the loss of friends. I didn't even like being touched by other people. The daily routine (rise at six, wash, line up for medication, eat, work, go to bed) suited me. I was alone in this life except for my voices and imagination. *That's just the way I want it,* I told myself.

The doctors grew concerned about my depressive state. "We can try giving him antidepressant medicines, and if they don't work, we can go to shock treatments," they said in front of me, the invisible man. Oh, but I could hear . . . and so could my voices.

Shock treatments, Kenny. . . . Electric volts going through your brain and leaving you senseless. How does that sound to you? . . . You should have electrocuted yourself in the shower the way we told you to, long, long ago. Now somebody else is going to have to do the job. . . . You're really in for it now.

Try as I might, I could not make the necessary changes in behavior, could not perk up or become more affable, as the doctors wished. But if I did not change, I knew, they would only put me on new and different medications. And if those medicines failed to lift my spirits? The phrase *shock treatments* reverberated through my addled brain. I had seen patients after they'd been given electroconvulsive therapy (ECT). They looked like zombies, and some of those I knew had lost their memories. Though they and I had spoken before, after treatment they no longer remembered me.

There was only one way I knew to avoid this dreaded fate: leave the hospital. And so, one winter morning, I did just that. Dressed in fresh clothes, good shoes, and a warm winter coat chosen from the secondhand bin, I left the main building, walked past the workshop, quit the hospital grounds, and just kept going.

I wasn't gone more than a week when the voices ordered me to take some rope that I'd found along the road, tie a noose, and hang myself from a tree. *What are you waiting for?* they asked after I'd located an accessible, hefty tree limb and managed to toss the rope over, then secure it. What indeed? *Get up there and stick your neck in the noose.*

Several times I tried to follow their commands, but I couldn't get the noose to support my six-foot, 170-pound body. The last attempt ended when I fell, banged my head on a stone, and wound up in a medical hospital.

What's your name?" I saw a blurred form and tried to make the speaker out. White uniform, peaked white cap. Oh, a nurse.

"You didn't have any identification on you, so we can't notify your family that you're here," she explained. "You took a fall and have a concussion. Some kids found you and summoned a police officer, who had you brought here." She nodded toward the door, and I noticed the officer. Again she asked, "Can you tell me your name?"

I lay there and said nothing. Nor did I respond to the doctor who next entered or to the psychiatrist who'd been called in on a consult. I was too sedated to speak. I also was tired—tired of hospitals, doctors, nurses, aides, social workers, security officers, kitchen staff. I was tired of talking, and so I remained mute.

"Well, son, your fingerprints drew a blank," said the psychiatrist after several visits during which I'd continued to hold my tongue. "Apparently, you're not wanted for anything, and you don't fit the description of anyone who's been reported as a runaway or missing person. If we can't figure out who you are, we will have to transfer you to Westboro State Hospital. Believe me, you don't want that. Now tell me who you are and where we can reach your family."

My silence bought a ride to Westboro, about forty miles west of Boston, where I was admitted as a "John Doe" and assigned to yet another locked and violent ward. Although I still spoke to no one (leading one doctor to describe me as *catatonic*), I growled. I now carried myself in a way that said clearly: DON'T MESS WITH ME. It mattered little to me what hospital or ward I was in, they were all part of the same system. And so was I. In my early twenties, I had become an institutionalized man.

I even had a new name. "Shannon Steele," I said to one of the attendants at Westboro about two weeks after I arrived. "That's my name." For one thing, I was worried that if people knew my real name, they'd soon learn that I'd eloped from Metropolitan; for another, I no longer wanted to be Kenny Steele. Thereafter, I used K. Shannon Steele as my official name and asked people to call me Shannon.

My life story would soon undergo further revision. Asked for the umpteenth time how and where the hospital could contact my family, I was amazed one day to hear myself reply, "My parents died in an airplane crash. I've been on my own since the age of eighteen." My voices had said often enough that I was dead to my parents; now they would be dead to me.

The voices would not let me get away with this. *You meant to say that* you're *the one who's going to die, didn't you, Kenny? Your family is alive . . . alive and thriving, as you well know. Your parents have Joey, a son they can be proud of. He doesn't have to change his name. He doesn't have to hide . . . and you do.*

Now where in Ireland did your people come from?" Patricia McCarthy, R.N., asked me. A slim woman who stood several inches below me, Nurse McCarthy had curly auburn hair, hazel eyes, an Ivory soap complexion that you could almost smell, and a smile that would brighten any room she entered. She looked to be in her early thirties—older than I was but not old enough to be my mother.

"What makes you think they came from Ireland?" I asked.

"And why else would they have named you Shannon?" she answered.

I smiled. I couldn't believe it—I actually smiled back in response.

"So you think I'm funny, do you?" she said.

I not only thought Nurse McCarthy funny, I thought she was the loveliest woman I had ever seen. And the nicest. I found myself looking forward to the times when she would be on duty, so we could talk. She never pried into my life, and so I felt free to share bits and pieces of it with her, like two friends having a conversation. As I opened up to her, I became more relaxed with others as well. Nurse McCarthy noticed the change. "One of these days, Shannon my lad, you may even be able to transfer from here to a halfway house on the grounds," she told me one day.

Halfway house? The Westboro campus, she explained, was made up of large buildings, like the one I was in, and smaller group homes—halfway houses—where patients lived more independently. The point of the program was to encourage residents to make their way back into the community on their own steam and to gain the skills needed to maintain a life outside the system. Many had jobs in Westboro or nearby towns and villages. The idea of doing something useful took hold of me. I quickly became a model patient and, with Nurse McCarthy's support and advocacy, soon made the transfer.

The halfway house I entered was a sprawling place with many bedrooms, a large kitchen and dining area, and a common room. I shared a bedroom with Wally, a nice enough guy who had an off-grounds job at a gas station and was learning to be a mechanic. In the beginning, at least, I was still expected to return to the main building each day for my medication and to meet with my doctor and nurse. In due course, I would pick up a month's supply of meds at the hospital and be responsible for my own compliance.

Each resident also had an in-house task; mine was to assist a fellow patient, Shirley, who prepared the group's meals. It didn't take long for me to realize that Shirley couldn't cook—not only that, but her sanitary habits left a lot to be desired. I paled as I watched her sink her dirty hands and filthy fingernails into the chopped meat, twisting and pounding it into a loaf. When I spoke to her about it, she said, "But look how clean my nails come out." Suffice it to say that I, who had survived on trash-can scraps, would not eat any food that Shirley had handled.

When I raised the matter at a house meeting, all the residents (but Shirley) agreed that something needed to be done, and they elected me cook. Since I'd been the one who'd complained, I felt that I had to rise to the challenge. I spent most of that night and the following days reading the few cookbooks that were in the kitchen. People shared their recipes with me, and I kind of learned as I went along. None of the residents complained. Indeed, some evenings they even applauded.

The outside job I coveted was that of an orderly. I'd enjoyed being with the older people during my stay in the infirmary following the rape and hospitalization and thought that I could not only manage that job, but also make a difference. Nurse McCarthy brought me books on how to handle a job interview (dress neatly, arrive promptly, sit up straight, and look directly at the interviewer). She spoke about something called a *résumé* and helped me prepare one, suggesting that I start by writing my current position, head cook at the halfway house, at the top. She also had me list my volunteer work with the elderly at Harlem Valley State Hospital, as well as my job at Fairchild Publications. I wrote that I had a high school diploma. Nurse McCarthy didn't know that was false. My voices did, and they called me a liar. *You will fail, just as you did at Fairchild,* they said. But the halfway house residents and Nurse McCarthy were giving me a different message. They told me I could do it, and so I was able to set aside the taunts of the evil voices. I felt hopeful and ready.

Any request to seek work outside the house had to be made to the residents. Three months passed before my doctor would allow me to raise the issue at a house meeting. I received the group's unanimous approval. Even Shirley voted in my favor. Now it was up to me to find the job. I wrote to a nursing home in the area and was given an appointment for an interview. The responsibility for getting there and back was mine as well. On the scheduled day, I hitchhiked the four miles to the facility, arriving early. "Miss Benton, the assistant director of nursing, will be with you shortly," said the receptionist after I carefully read and filled out the job application she had handed me. (Nurse McCarthy's voice was in my ear: "Don't write *See résumé* on the application," she had counseled me. "Answer every question they ask.")

Miss Benton didn't keep me waiting. "So you're Mr. Steele," she said, indicating a chair before her desk.

"Yes, ma'am," I said, smiling broadly and maintaining eye contact as I took my seat. In answer to her questions, I spoke of my genuine feeling for the elderly and gave examples of how I had interacted with the people in the infirmary.

"Do you think you could handle bathing men who are incontinent?" she asked.

I wasn't sure what her question meant. "Miss Benton, I think *incontinent* means that the men lose control of their bladder or bowels, is that right?" I asked.

"Very good," she said, smiling broadly. I told her I could manage that and, in answer to other questions posed to me, said that I would work "any" shifts—double shifts, back-to-back, graveyard. The decisions were mine to make; I just had to phone "home" if I planned to work late. That's what I liked about the halfway house. They treated the residents like grown-ups.

"Okay, I'll get in touch with Mrs. Peele, the nurse who requested an orderly," Miss Benton said. "She should be calling you in a day or two to schedule a second interview." Miss Benton wished me good luck and handed me some papers describing the work rules and benefits at the nursing home.

Five very long days passed before I received a call from Mrs. Peele. I arrived for our meeting with high hopes and a nobody's-going-to-say-no-to-me attitude, except that somebody did. "No, I need someone older, more patient, and much more experienced," Mrs. Peele told me. I was devastated. As I headed home, I wondered how I was going to break the news to Nurse McCarthy and my fellow residents.

I opened the door to the halfway house slowly. "Congratulations," everyone called at the top of their lungs. Nurse McCarthy was there, her warm smile enveloping me.

"Stop!" I shouted above the din. "You're all wonderful, but I didn't get the job. I was too inexperienced."

"Yes, you did," said Nurse McCarthy. "Miss Benton phoned here and left you a message: You start work tomorrow . . . as a cook!"

I returned Miss Benton's call. She confirmed my employment, and added that she also had signed me up for a basic nurse's aide course where, among other things, I'd be taught to take blood pressure, perform CPR (cardiopulmonary resuscitation), and do the Heimlich maneuver—in case people choked on their food.

Now we could celebrate. As I cut the cake that my halfway house friends had prepared for me, Nurse McCarthy asked if she could have the honor of cutting the second piece. "I have good news, too," she told us. "I'm expecting a baby." I looked at her. How could I not have seen? But the voices kept me so self-centered that I often failed to notice important things happening to the people around me. I felt happy for her, happy for me, genuinely, generally happy.

I was now on Trilafon, the first antipsychotic medication that didn't give me horrible side effects. (Like so many mentally ill patients, I became my own doctor, adjusting the doses of my medications; in this case, I took half the measurement that my doctor prescribed.) The drug seemed to slow the voices down, but I couldn't be sure of cause and effect. Whenever I was deeply immersed in something (like my efforts to prepare for, and get, a job at the nursing home) or engaged with people I trusted, the voices lost their commanding influence on me. Unfortunately, these periods never lasted very long because the voices were always waiting in the dark, prepared to take advantage of any opportunity, any slight break in my confidence, when they would take over and aim me toward self-destruction.

Still, it was the stable periods, times when I was most productive, that built my self-esteem and helped balance the down times. And so it is with so many of us who struggle with schizophrenia and other mental illnesses. That's one of the reasons I feel so strongly about the need to be given meaningful work instead of the make-busy tasks or rote assignments that make up the bulk of what we are offered. If people are treated as capable, they often surprise everyone and live up to expectations.

I had been working in the kitchen at the nursing home for two weeks, preparing food and helping to feed patients, when I was called to the office of Mrs. Adams, the director of nurses. She told me that people had been pleased with my work and that the staff had especially noted my success in feeding the most difficult patients. Henceforward, I would work one shift in the kitchen, another as an orderly, reporting to Mrs. Peele. Was that okay with me?

The job of orderly suited me. I liked the routine—bathing and dressing "my men," cleaning and making their beds. As I worked, I would tell them stories I had read in books and listen to the tales they would tell about their own lives. When time permitted, I would read to them. They liked biographies about men who had been active when they, too, were in their prime—heroes like Charles Lindbergh or General MacArthur, writers like Jack London and Ernest Hemingway. My lunches were for the ladies, whom I called "my beauties." They, too, liked me to read to them, but they preferred the works of Laura Ingalls Wilder or Lucy Maud Montgomery, author of *Anne of Green Gables*. I worked double shifts routinely—sometimes sleeping the third shift on a cot in the nursing home—and never complained. I had a home, friends, a job I enjoyed, and was respected for my skills. This period of my life, lasting eight months, was the closest I would come, for decades, to living anything close to a normal life.

One evening, I returned from work to find a message to phone Nurse McCarthy's ward. The news was bad, said the person who took my call. "Nurse McCarthy was attacked by a new admission," she told me, "and the baby was born prematurely. Both mother and child are hospitalized and in critical condition. We thought you would want to know." I sobbed, certain that my demons had caused this, too.

Days turned to weeks as I waited for word of my friend's condition. I threw myself into my work, filling in for any employee who called in sick, just so I wouldn't have to think. At long last, Miss Benton called me to her office. "We've had news," she said. "Fortunately, Nurse McCarthy will recover. The bad news is that the baby lived only three weeks."

The voices rained down upon me from all sides. *If it weren't for you, Nurse McCarthy would never have lost her baby.*

She was thinking of taking time off for the pregnancy, but then you came along. She stayed because of you . . . because you kept her here.

It was another boy, you know.

How many more people will you hurt? You must die so that others can live. When are you finally going to do our bidding? Suicide's the only answer.

It was one of the worst psychotic storms of my life. I was bombarded by the voices and overcome by self-loathing. Here I'd been trying so hard to achieve some kind of useful life, but every attempt resulted in disaster and I was back where I started: damned. I *had* to be damned to hell, just as my grandmother had prophesied when I told her about my voices. Damned to wander the world a loner. I returned to the halfway house, packed what few things I could carry, pocketed my small savings, and once more started walking. It was the only way I knew to handle a problem—flee from it.

On the road, I slept mostly in public toilets along interstate highways, where I was often forced to fight off the predators who rob and assault the homeless mentally ill. Autumn was turning to winter. I began to hitchhike again, this time catching a ride with a man driving a large tractor-trailer to Chicago. A redheaded guy whose worn jeans were held in place by wide suspenders over a plaid flannel shirt, the driver told me that there would be a price for the ride. In return for "certain sexual favors"—that's how he put it—he would provide safe passage, plus food and drink. I didn't have to ask what he meant: Ted and Nick had taught me well.

I hoisted myself up to the cab, and we were off. Along the way, "Red" introduced me to vodka, and I soon discovered the numbing relief that alcohol could bring to a mind searching for forgetfulness. He kept the radio on much of the time, and the vodka helped dull the voices that emanated from it—voices that now had even more to rail about.

At last we reached Chicago. Gusts blew across Lake Michigan into a city that struck me as more intimidating than Boston but less inviting than New York. Shivering, I pulled the collar of my jacket up and looked about me, wondering in which direction to head. I felt fearfully alone and vulnerable.

"I know places you can stay, boy, and people who will put you up for a while if you do with them what you did with me," Red said. "I've got friends clear across this country."

There you go again, Kenny. Once a ho, always a ho. Is this what you're struggling to live for? No, I told the voices, but I *was* struggling to live, and satisfying men's desires was preferable to selling drugs or committing robberies—two other opportunities that had been offered me during my wanderings and that I'd rejected. I told Red I'd be grateful for his assistance.

He paid for a room at the kind of motel that charges by the hour and, to my delight, allowed me to enjoy a night's sleep. The next morning, Red took me to a barbershop, where a man cut my hair short and a lady soaked and clipped my fingernails. Then we were off to a clothing store, where I was outfitted with slacks, sports coats, shoes—"the latest duds," Red called them. I would be "Cinderfella" for a night or two, he told me, until he found me a prince.

That night we went to a gay nightclub named the Napoleon Club, probably because of all the short, portly, balding men who seemed to be its principal patrons. There were also tall young men like myself whose attire ranged from formal to casual: From the look of us, we could have been college students or executive trainees—young men who had yet to make their mark on life. But I *was* marked. It didn't take long before I was approached by a nice-looking man whom I guessed to be in his early thirties. He stood about my height, had straight black hair that he wore short, a black mustache, and dark, deep-set eyes that reminded me of the actor Omar Sharif. His name was Karl, he said (I told him mine was Shannon), and asked if I would join him in the parlor, where it was quiet.

We sat together for a long time; mostly, Karl talked and I listened. He told me that he'd attended college and business school, both at Harvard, and had worked in his father's business until recently. He said that his family owned a home in Wheaton, Illinois, but that he lived in an apartment in the city. Finally, he invited me to go home with him—not just for the night, but to move in with him; if we got along, he said, he would take care of me.

I said I had to speak to Red. At the start of the long drive from Massachusetts to Chicago, I'd told Red about having been raped, making clear to him that there were strict limits to what I would do and, more importantly, what I would not allow to be done to me in a sexual relationship. Red had respected those boundaries. Now I asked him to make them clear to Karl. The two men spoke briefly, then Red wished me well. "You don't have to pay me back for the duds, kid," were his parting words to me. "Everything's been taken care of."

And so I moved into Karl's apartment on one of the upper floors of a high-rise on Lake Shore Drive. It had wraparound windows, furniture of polished wood, deep beige carpets, and glass tables that gleamed beneath the indirect lighting. There was a working fireplace in the living room. Karl showed me to my bedroom; it was larger than the entire first floor of my childhood home, and it came with a private bathroom. But it was the amazing view of the city that most commanded my attention—that and the roaring, fierce voices that came at me now in a very big way, multiplying in number and increasing in volume.

Look at the buildings, the tall, tall buildings, they ordered in chorus. *Smart, Kenny. Really smart to get this fag to take you to one of the tallest ones. . . . Look at the terrace, Kenny. You don't have to climb to the top of a very tall building. You're already here. See how easy it will be? You can just step out onto that terrace and make the leap you should have taken long ago. . . . This is where you will end your life, in Chicago, the Windy City. . . . Jump! We'll watch the wind carry you away.*

Karl could not fail to see the look of horror on my face. He handed me a drink. I gulped it down, felt a burning in my throat, and asked for another. Three drinks succeeded in making the voices recede . . . like the ebbing of a wave that, moments before, had arrived in full force, roaring and crashing its way toward the shore.

Karl had more than three drinks—not just that night, but every night. He used to joke that most of his friends were over twenty years old, and in time he introduced me to some of them: Jack Daniel, Johnny Walker, and Jim Beam. They helped him forget, he said. I wondered briefly if he, too, might be schizophrenic, but I soon discovered that his demons were of a different nature.

What plagued Karl was the devastating loss of his mother and father, who were killed in a car crash when rounding a notoriously dangerous S curve on Lake Shore Drive, less than a mile from his place. An only son, Karl had inherited the family business, for which he'd been groomed from day one.

Since the accident, however, he couldn't bear to walk into the factory and, for the most part, left the running of the company to others while he sought solace in dimly lit bars, making friends out of strangers.

"Karl can't stand being alone," a patron at one of the places that we frequented told me one evening, adding, "He's constantly picking up young guys, letting them stay with him, and getting ripped off. One even threatened him with a weapon."

That explained a lot of things—for example, the fact that Karl yearned for companionship more than he wanted sex. But he liked to pretend to others that we were ardent lovers, and I went along with the ruse. He was a good and generous companion, and I came to care for him deeply.

One day, Karl told me that he had to make a business trip to Denver and asked if I wanted to come along. Sure, I said. This would be my first flight—and we were going first-class, no less. My voices came along for the ride. *So you think the clouds are beautiful, do you?* they said. *Well, take a good look at them, because this is as close to heaven as you will ever get.* The stewardess offered me another drink. "Yes, thank you," I said, and took two small bottles of whiskey, which I downed quickly.

The city of Denver lies on a kind of plain that looks out at the Rocky Mountains—a sight so awesome to this boy from the East, I thought at first it must be a hallucination. Karl had booked us a room at the elegant Brown Palace Hotel, which gleamed of onyx and marble. We stayed for three days, spending most of the time at a bar named The Court Jester, a popular spot where Karl was known. His drinking grew increasingly worse, and I didn't know how to stop him. The fourth morning, Karl announced that he had business in town. "Here," he said, putting an arm around my shoulders before handing me some money. "Go shopping and enjoy the city." I thought that odd, since Karl usually liked to know just where I was—and where I was, from the moment we met, was with him. I did his bidding.

Later that afternoon, I returned to the hotel expecting to freshen up and head out, with Karl, for the evening. "Sorry," said the desk clerk when I requested the key to our room. Karl had checked out. "Your luggage has been stored with us," said the clerk. "Do you want to retrieve it now?"

Did I want . . . what? I asked the clerk to check again, but he told me that there was no mistake. He'd been on duty when Karl had paid the bill and gone. Not once, but at least a half dozen times, I phoned Karl's number in Chicago. No one answered. I pondered my next move. Should I return to Chicago and head back to the apartment? I wanted the life I'd been leading. I wanted Karl.

Sure he left you, said the voices. *You were just a fling. Who could care about you?* They began laughing hysterically. I needed to quiet them so I could plan my next move. "Will you hold my luggage for a few days?" I asked the desk clerk.

"There are lockers at the Greyhound bus terminal," he answered.

I lugged my suitcases from the hotel to the terminal, a distance of about half a mile, and located the lockers. As I stowed my stuff inside, a younger Ken flashed before my eyes—a teenager who had placed his trunk for overnight safekeeping in Grand Central Station. I remembered the owner of that baggage as a boy who had been filled with hopes and dreams, and I saw myself now as someone who was as trashed and abandoned as that long-lost trunk. I slumped on a bench in the terminal and cried bitterly, mourning the loss of myself: the innocent and bright youth I once was and the worthwhile man I might have become. Now, as before, a predator approached me. "Need some help, kid?" he said. I instantly jumped to my feet, glared at the approaching stranger with fierce red eyes, and ran out of the station, heading straight for The Court Jester to find my friend vodka.

As the drink took effect, I sank into a deeper and deeper depression. Now, even *without* the voices nudging me on, suicide became a serious option, a way out of the sorrow and the sordidness. I felt it as a heavy weight, dragging me down to the depths where demons reside. I did not want to be picked up by anyone at the bar that night. I had no stomach for it. I left, searching for a secluded spot to rest. The voices came back as the alcohol wore off, their message (as always) a relentless mix of disdain and despotism—ordering me to do away with myself.

Then I did the most extraordinary thing. *On my own*, I went to the emergency room of a hospital—no ambulance, police, or drama of any kind brought me there—and told the receptionist that I needed to see a doctor. She asked what was wrong. "I'm feeling depressed," I said. She asked if I had insurance, and I replied that I didn't. She handed me a form and asked me to fill it out. Then I waited.

Eventually, a nurse called my name and showed me to an office, where she took my temperature, blood pressure, and pulse, then asked why I was there. Again I said, "I'm very depressed."

"You know," she said, having smelled my breath, "alcohol is a depressant." I simply stared at her. How could I make her understand the seriousness of my situation? "Do you have suicidal ideation?" she asked me.

"I don't know what that means," I told her, "but I have voices telling me to jump off buildings and to cut my throat." She made me promise not to leave the office while she arranged for a doctor to see me. Then she left, briefly, saying, "A resident will be here soon. Meanwhile, there's some medicine that can help you with your feelings." I told her I did well on Trilafon, but she said the doctor had ordered a different type of medication. Before I even knew it, she had given me a shot of something that put me to sleep.

When the doctor arrived, he shook me awake and asked me questions about what day of the month it was, who was the president, and what was meant by the saying "People in glass houses shouldn't throw stones." There's a standard drill that psychiatrists, nurses, and social workers use to determine the extent of your dementia. It's a useful screening device, I know, but when you're asked these questions time and again, as I was, it feels like they're toying with you; it's an insult to your intelligence. Sometimes I knew the month; sometimes I didn't. Sometimes I knew and wouldn't say.

I told the doctor about the overwhelming feeling of depression I was experiencing. In answer to his questions, I also told him of my previous hospitalizations for mental illness. He arranged to have me taken by ambulance to Fort Logan Mental Health Center. I asked him to make sure that I wouldn't be placed in restraints since I was entering voluntarily, and he agreed, but when the drivers arrived, they immediately restrained me in four-point straps, immobilizing my arms and legs. In answer to my protests, they said it was a company requirement. They also insisted that I be further medicated. I wondered whether turning myself in had been the right decision. I think I was given Thorazine, because I became heavily sedated and once again felt as if I were jumping out of my skin.

Dale Woods was the social worker assigned to me at the hospital. Thin, short, with curly blond hair, Mr. Woods walked with a pronounced limp. He nodded in understanding when I explained my symptoms. "My older sister hears voices," he said. "Like you, she's often been hospitalized after serious suicide attempts." Mr. Woods was the only professional I'd met in the system who revealed a family connection to someone who was schizophrenic. This disclosure totally disarmed me. I spoke to him for more than two and a half hours that first time. Of course I told him about Karl's abandoning me, which had led to this latest, deepest depression.

"We need to find out about Karl," Mr. Woods said. He offered to call the Brown Palace Hotel to confirm the dates of our stay, after which he would phone Karl in Chicago, with my permission. I agreed. When Mr. Woods came to see me the next afternoon, I knew at once that something was wrong. He seemed to drag himself into the room reluctantly. His limp was more pronounced. "Your friend Karl committed suicide," he said, almost in a whisper. "He took an overdose of sleeping pills and alcohol."

I couldn't find words to respond. Instead, I looked out a window at some trees swaying from the strength of the gusting wind. "He left a suicide note," Mr. Woods went on. "He said he was sorry, but he couldn't continue to live with the loss of his parents." He paused, allowing me time to take in the sense of what I'd just been told. "You were mentioned, too," said Mr. Woods. "Karl said he was sorry he stranded you, but he was sure that you were resilient enough to make it on your own."

I didn't cry. In the days and weeks that followed, Mr. Woods helped me work through my grief. He gave me a copy of Elisabeth Kubler-Ross's book *On Death and Dying,* and I began the process of accepting Karl's suicide. But I continued to avoid and deny my loss of myself (the person I could have been) to my disease.

"'Mr. Steele has made vast improvements in his affect and attitude toward life, no longer posing a danger to himself,'" Mr. Woods read aloud to me from the notes he was making on my chart in preparation for my discharge from the hospital. I'd told him that I wanted to live in a halfway house and look for a job again. He explained that the job came first here; once I had one, I needed to seek acceptance at one of the halfway houses that had a vacancy.

I applied for the job of orderly or cook at four nursing homes in the area. At one, I was quickly called back for a second interview. They had reached my former employer, the nursing home near the Westboro campus, and received a good reference. I was hired as an orderly. There was other good news for me. Apparently, I'd left my former post before receiving my last paycheck. I had but to call with my current address and the money would be forwarded.

Job in hand, I applied and was accepted for admittance to a halfway house. I had mixed feelings about leaving the hospital—the first where I had voluntarily sought help. Although my depression had lifted enough for me to be able to manage a job, the therapy sessions with Mr. Woods led me to a deeper awareness of the hopelessness of my situation. No matter what advances I fought long and hard to make, the ever-present voices had the power to reverse my efforts. Medications that managed to quell them also sedated me to the point that I couldn't walk and talk at the same time. Alcohol, which could quiet the voices, posed a real danger of further complicating my already uncontrollable life.

Mr. Woods encouraged me to take a high school equivalency exam, earn my diploma, and go on to nursing school. But the voices said no. Vociferously. *You'll flunk the test, Kenny,* I heard. *You didn't get through high school the first time, and you won't make it now. . . . You're a loser, a mental misfit who should have been aborted.*

Try as I did to bury my deepening sorrow, I soon found myself repeating an all-too-familiar pattern. One night, I walked away from house, job, and therapist for no discernible reason except that the voices told me to do it. They were a part of me, like the hair on my head, the nails on my fingers. I needed to prove they were right, to show that I *was* a failure at everything.

I spent about a week on the streets of Denver, hunched in doorways, at times curled beneath boxes soaked from a steady, cold rain. Then I hit the road, drifting like a scrap of paper in whatever direction the wind might take me. The voices wanted me to walk into heavy, fast-moving traffic and get hit by a truck.

A big truck will squash you like a wild rabbit or a skunk, they told me. *You're too insignificant to bring harm to the*

driver of one of the large eighteen-wheelers, and you know it.
Pick a big, fast-moving truck, Kenny, and it will all be over.

I walked for a day and a half along Highway 25, waiting for the right-sized truck and the right moment to throw myself in front of it (when there'd be no other traffic and, therefore, no possibility of a pileup causing harm to anyone else). Eventually, a state trooper spotted me and pulled over. I was actively hallucinating. Once more through the revolving door. I soon found myself in restraints again, being taken by ambulance to yet another facility.

Pueblo State Hospital in Pueblo, Colorado, is a place to revisit only in memory—and even then, briefly. Seclusion here was not a room, but a closet. It felt as if they had opened a large drawer in a wall, containing a mattress, placed me inside (still in restraints), and closed the drawer. The top of the drawer was open but covered by a thick metal screen. Metal bars ran horizontally across the space, preventing me from standing up even if I had managed to extricate myself from the restraints. Vents on the sides of the drawer permitted air to enter. To this day, I don't know if the drawer image was true or one drawn for me by the voices that, during this period, came close to smothering me in sound. I do know that I'd never before been afraid of being in enclosed places; after I left Pueblo, I was terrified of them and remain so to this day.

The ward to which I was eventually assigned was full of the most dangerous patients, and they attacked in groups. Behind the safety of their glass-paned nursing station, staff members could be seen smiling and laughing as patients pummeled one another. It seemed to me that some aides even wagered on winners and losers. I *had* to get out of this place. All avenues were blocked but one.

I would be here for a very long time, I was told, unless . . . Unless I could get my family to agree to have me return to Connecticut, to return home.

{6}

Closing Other Doors

TEN YEARS HAD PASSED since I'd last seen or spoken to my parents. There were times when I had been hospitalized just a few hours' drive from their home, yet they hadn't visited or even phoned me. Why should I think they would now intercede, with almost a decade and half a country's distance between us? I agonized over whether to contact them. One thing was clear: They were my *only* means of getting out of the hell that was Pueblo State Hospital. And so one day, my fingers shaking, I dialed home. A recorded message said that the number had been changed and the new number was unlisted.

I remembered the phone number of Aunt Joan, my father's older sister, and tried that. After two rings, my aunt answered. Though I'd placed the call, I was startled by hearing a voice from my past on the other end of the line. "Please call my parents," I asked her, "and give them the number of this pay phone. I'll be waiting to hear from them." She agreed to deliver the message. I thanked her and hung up.

A patient wanted to make a call. I tried to explain the situation, but he shoved me aside, deposited a coin, and began dialing his number. I stood a few feet away. He dropped the receiver, letting it dangle from the call box while he walked up to me and told me to back off . . . or else. I retreated. The minute he finished his conversation, I resumed my sentry position at the phone. Another patient approached. This time, I played the tough guy. "I'm waiting for a very important call," I announced, deepening my voice and glaring at him. "If you want to use this phone right away, you'll have to go through me to get it." Our eyes met, and I thought we were about to get into a battle when he blinked and shuffled off.

A few minutes later, the phone rang. I picked up the receiver and heard my father on the other end of the line. "Is Kenny Steele there?" His voice was little changed. I felt myself shaking.

"This is Ken," I said. I couldn't recall the last time I had answered to that name.

The first thing my dad asked was why I had bothered my aunt. I told him that his own number was unlisted and it was the only way I could get to him. I asked about the family. He said that he, my mother, and brother were fine. "And Grandma?" I asked. That's when I learned that my beloved grandmother had died more than a year earlier, on August 22, 1974, a few weeks before her eighty-seventh birthday. I went silent, but my father reminded me that this was a long-distance call. What did I want?

I gulped, dove in, and told him where I was, that I desperately wanted to leave and needed his help. He had to consent to my coming back home. He paused, then said my mother would speak with me. I told my mom how terrible I felt about Grandma's death. She began to cry. Dad took the phone back and said my brother would like to talk to me. My brother! The boy who got on sounded like a young man. He said hi, asked how I was, and I said fine, then asked him how he was. It was textbook small talk. Then my father got on the line again. "Do you need any money?" he asked. I didn't need any money, I said; I'd already told him what I needed. He said the call was expensive and he had to go. I said good-bye and he hung up.

The phone call and the news of Grandma's death hit me like a one-two punch. *She's gone,* said my voices. *Your grandma's gone to heaven. Fat chance you have of seeing her again.* The voices also made a fuss about my brother: *Boy, that Joey's a big kid now. . . . He's fine, didn't you hear that? Nothing's wrong with Joey. . . . You told him you were fine, too. You know you're not fine, Kenny. You lied again. Liars go to hell. You're in a living hell, and you're going to stay here.*

Filled with pain and fury, I felt a need to strike out at the world. I began to roam the area looking for fights. Challenging the most dangerous men on the violent ward, I managed to get involved in two serious scuffles before day's end. I expected these guys to hurt me, and I wanted them to do their worst. I was tired of hurting so much inside. The voices were right. I should have taken my life years ago. If I couldn't manage it, maybe I could incite one of the groups here to do the deed for me. Once I took this attitude, however, I became the feared one. These guys wouldn't kill me; they backed away when I walked by.

"Steele!" I heard my name shouted. "Telephone!"

My father was on the line. "Your brother wants to know you," he said bluntly. "Tell me where you are and what I have to do to get you out of there."

"Please wait a minute," I said to my dad. I put down the receiver and moved as if in a trance. Eleven steps to the nurses' station. I knocked on the glass window and asked the person on duty, "Can you speak to my father, please?" She emerged from her cubicle and went quickly to the phone. I stood by as the staff member told my father who to contact about "Shannon's" release. Then she handed me the receiver.

"Who's Shannon?" asked my father.

"It's too long a story to go into right now," I said, adding, "And this is a long-distance call." I still knew what buttons to push.

"Right," said my dad. He told me that he would do what was needed to get me back home. Even as I thanked him, I wanted to cry "Stop!" at the top of my lungs. Something inside me knew that this was wrong, that I shouldn't go home again. But my voices were having a field day with the news. *Kenny's going home to meet his younger brother,* they called out gleefully. *Oh, how sweet. We're going to meet Joey, the good kid. We can't wait, can't wait....*

The fact that my voices were cheering on my return home only heightened my concern.

The state of Colorado was so pleased to have someone else assume the cost of my care, it even provided me with one-way fare from Denver's Stapleton International Airport to Bradley Field in Hartford, Connecticut, where my parents were to meet me. But first, I had to be made presentable. My hair, worn long in the hospital, was cut to a respectable length. My face had paled—the result of institutional living. Miraculously, my suitcases had been retrieved from the halfway house where I'd gone to live upon leaving Fort Logan Mental Health Center. For the journey home, I selected a dark brown shirt and pants and a brown paisley tie—one that Karl had especially liked. I was driven to the airport by state van. Two attendants escorted me to the gate and made sure that I boarded. It was a nonstop flight.

Tarred and feathered out of town, said my voices, *but at least they kicked you out in style.*

I wondered if my parents would recognize me. My appearance had changed a lot in ten years. But not enough. My father met me at the gate, and we recognized each other instantly. Strangers would have guessed we were kin. Dad accompanied me to the baggage claim area. He insisted on carrying both suitcases to the parking lot, where we located his green Toyota station wagon. Inside sat my mom. When I first saw her, it took my breath away because she so closely resembled my grandmother.

We drove the hour and a quarter west along Route 84 to Prospect, alternating silence with awkward conversation. Dad brought me up-to-date on the status of his Pittsburgh teams. Mom said that Joey was eager to meet me. I asked them to tell me more about Joey. This was clearly a welcome topic. My parents spoke glowingly about his good nature. They told me that he loved sports, excelling in both football and baseball. They didn't ask about my life, and I didn't ask about Grandma's final days. We kept the talk safe.

The house seemed even smaller than I remembered. Inside there were changes. The room that had been occupied by Grandma was now my parents' bedroom, while their room was used for storage. Joey had my old room. The basement had been converted to a family room with a sofa, exercise equipment, a TV set, and an old stereo that I'd received as a gift so many Christmases ago. This room also would serve as my bedroom, I was told.

Then Joey arrived. When I first set eyes on my brother, it was like looking into a mirror at my own image when I was his age. The Steele men all look alike. But the similarity stopped right there. Joey greeted me awkwardly and asked if I wanted to play an electronic football game with him after dinner. I said I was a little tired and asked if we could play the next day. Joey asked about the plane I'd flown on and seemed disappointed that I didn't remember what model it was. He asked if I'd seen any recent ball games. He knew every player's statistics and shared them with me, trying to gain my approval. I listened, fascinated by this creature—the me my parents wanted. He talked throughout dinner. Then he prepared for bed. It was a school night, after all, our father reminded him.

I asked my mother if I could look through Grandma's family album. She said she would join me. We turned the pages, looking at photographs of my grandmother as she grew from a young girl in Pennsylvania to the beautiful bride of a man who managed a fruit farm, then to a wise and adored mother of four and grandmother of sixteen. My mother turned to me and said, in an unusual expression of kindness, "You were always her favorite grandchild, you know. 'My special one' is what she called you." She added, "Your grandmother was the best friend you ever had." I knew that. Back once again in the home where we had lived together, holding Grandma's life's record in my hands, I felt how great was my loss.

I needed air. It was fall, a cool breeze was blowing in from Canada, and I thought a brisk walk would be invigorating. "I'm going out for a while," I announced. My father gave me a look that lasted long enough to make his point: I was under surveillance. He'd be the one to decide if my behavior merited the granting of ground privileges here.

"Okay," he said curtly. "But be back in fifteen minutes, that's it."

I walked to the small recreation area just up the street from our home, sat in the bleachers of the football field, and I cried. No question about it, coming home had been a mistake. This was where the voices had first visited me, and they were still present—only more powerful. They continued to dominate my life, leaving me in ruins time and again. A feeling of dread overwhelmed me. I didn't want to fall apart here with my family. I would visit for a few days, thank my folks for their hospitality, shake my brother's hand, and then move on without fuss or mess. That was my plan.

Events took a different turn.

For the first few days of my visit, the voices were subdued—quietly chatting in the background like the gentle hubbub created by Saturday shoppers at the mall: clearly there, but not intrusive. Pueblo State had supplied enough pills to get me through the first couple of weeks at home (by which time, they believed, I would have found a new doctor), but I took none of them. I was saving the pills for a new suicide plan, one that I'd begun plotting earlier that year after I overheard hospital attendants speaking about a young woman back East who had mixed psychiatric medications with alcohol and was then in a coma. They said she was being kept alive but was brain dead. I liked the idea of killing my brain and the voices and hallucinations that came from it.

In an effort to learn more about the incident, I visited the Prospect town library. ("Tell him not to come home late," said my father when my mother phoned him at work to see if I could leave the house.) There was a new librarian at the information desk. I asked if she remembered hearing about the young woman in the coma, providing what scant details I had of the incident. "Oh, you must mean Karen Ann Quinlan," she said at once. "It's so sad." She suggested that I read up on the story in newspaper editions from the period March through May 1975, directing me to the section where they were stored. Soon I had the information I needed. The medications used by Miss Quinlan were anti-anxiety agents, Valium and Librium. I needed to get hold of them.

It was growing dark when I got home, and my mother looked annoyed. "Sorry," I said. "You know I tend to lose myself in the library." I'd applied for a card, and in a few days I would take out Ken Kesey's *One Flew Over the Cuckoo's Nest,* a novel about mental illness that became an award-winning film starring Jack Nicholson. Kesey had nothing new to tell me. The territory was familiar.

My mother was preparing dinner, and I offered to help, explaining that I had earned my living as a cook. I think she believed it was another of my made-up stories. "I can manage better alone," she said, and so I retreated to my basement quarters, where I passed the time looking through a stack of records. With some surprise, I came upon *Stop the World, I Want to Get Off,* the last album I'd bought before leaving home. I must have been prescient way back then, for the title exactly described the way I was feeling now. I put the record on the turntable, pushed the PLAY button, and listened to Anthony Newley and the cast sing the songs of that hit musical.

Joey had come home from school and was in his room, doing his homework. Mom was cooking a pot roast. It was past seven when I heard my father's car in the driveway. The moment my father entered the house, Joey came flying down the stairs to welcome him and tell him all about how football practice had gone and report the coach's indecision about which position Joey should play.

"Quarterback is your position," said my father. "The coach will make you quarterback or he'll have to speak to me about it." At dinner, the talk moved from football to grades. Joey was an honor student, but my dad said he expected all A's and no more B's on the next report card. "You need to be a scholar-athlete," he told my brother, who nodded solemnly.

The meal over, my father asked me to join him outside on the back stairs. This was a first, and I wondered if his paternal benevolence now extended to me as well. I'd barely sat down when my father informed me that he'd managed to get me a job. "It's with a medical instrument manufacturer who needs quality assurance people," he said. "The plant is located in downtown Waterbury, so I'll be able to drop you off on my way to work, and you can take the bus home. You start Monday." Then he added his blessing: "It's a simple job, so you shouldn't have any trouble with it."

"Thanks," I said. I told him briefly about some of the assembly-line jobs I'd held over the years. He nodded approvingly.

"I want you and your brother to get to know each other," he said. "But I must warn you: The first time I see any strange behavior from you, you'll have to leave. Understood?"

"Yes." I then asked if I could see a doctor so that I could maintain my medication and therapy.

"The people at the hospital told me you needed to see a mental doctor," he answered, "and I'll ask around, but I don't want you bringing any of that kind of talk into the house. As soon as you get a paycheck, I'll expect you to pay for the doctor and the medication. Your mother and I will figure out what's fair for room and board, too."

Meeting adjourned.

And so I began a routine of work and home, where my parents pretty much left me alone. Joey approached winning me over as vigorously as he pursued excellence in sports, trying to engage me in one or another of his interests and enthusiasms. Even as I admired his determination in attempting to break through to this strange older brother, I resented the ease with which he seemed to be sailing through the rest of life. I said nothing about this to him, but I was difficult to reach and I sensed that he knew I was jealous.

The job wasn't bad. I wore a white jacket and cap, and I inspected medical instrument parts under a microscope to ensure that a particular electrical wire was correctly connected at both ends. As before, I found the repetitive nature of the work oddly soothing; it kept my voices and hallucinations under control. Soon I was working overtime and earning much more money. My father was pleased with me, although the added work meant that I wouldn't always make it home in time for dinner. Joey was glad that my father seemed less critical of my behavior. On the surface, then, life was calm.

Except that I hadn't abandoned my design to kill my brain.

The Ruler was happy with this. *This is the first intelligent idea you've had in a long time,* he told me. I could see his pointed red tongue licking his thin lips in pleasure, his sharp teeth and gleaming eyes. *Just swallow the pills and then drink yourself into oblivion. Eternal oblivion, that's what it's all about. Karen Ann Quinlan knows this. Soon you will know it, too.*

I'd begun seeing a psychiatrist in Waterbury, who prescribed Thorazine (to suppress my voices) and Librium (because I complained of feelings of anxiety). I had the prescriptions filled but didn't use either of the medications, saving them for the overdose that I planned to take. Then I discovered a bar near my workplace, where I would sometimes stop to have a drink or two at day's end. I confided to the bartender that I was feeling anxious. "I'd rather use medication than alcohol to calm me down," I said, "but I don't know where to get the stuff." One evening, he told me he could get Valium at a good price; and the next night, he sold me an entire bottle of the pills. *Here's to your successful dying,* the voices toasted me as I drank my beer. *This time, you will finally get it right.*

There was often alcohol on my breath on the nights when I came home late from work. My father asked me to stop drinking, but since I hadn't caused any disturbance (yet), he didn't forbid me a drink or two. I took that as permission. Even with several drinks under my belt, I could still hear the voices as they continued to shout invectives at me. But now I knew the day was coming when I would be rid of them and the world would be rid of me. Everybody would be happy.

One morning, I left for work with a pocketful of pills and all of my savings. (I'd just paid the doctor's bill and my parents for room and board, so the total didn't amount to much.) As always, my father dropped me off at the plant, but that day I didn't enter the building. When his car was out of sight, I walked in the direction of the bar and waited for it to open. I was the first customer. Calmly, I swallowed some Thorazine and a lot of the Librium and Valium (planning to finish them all during the course of the day), drinking it all down with a Jack Daniel's straight up with ice. More pills, more Jack Daniel's.

Then . . . blackout.

The events that followed are reconstructed from fragments of distorted memory and the accounts of others. I was thrown out of the bar and somehow made my way to the Waterbury train station. I don't know why I went there. Maybe I was trying to leave Waterbury. What I do remember, vaguely, is walking down the street *away* from the train station when I was chased down by two police officers in a cruiser. I ran and they followed, caught up with me, and savagely beat me. The next thing I recall was waking up in a jail cell. Two of my front teeth had been knocked out; another tooth was broken. My face was black, blue, purple, and red. My eyes were swollen; I saw out of slits. My head and entire body throbbed with pain. Charges had been made against me.

Someone must have phoned my home, for my father was present to post a bail bond that would get me out of jail that same night. With that accomplished, he drove his son the prisoner home. Not a word passed between us. Furious as my father was, he couldn't have hurt me more than I'd already hurt myself, more than I'd been injured by strangers, and he knew it. Joey was in bed by the time we arrived. My mother was shocked when she saw my condition. But not as upset as she soon would be.

"Kenny, come up here now!" she shouted down to the basement the next morning. My mother rarely raised her voice.

I jumped, or fell, off the sofa.

"Kenny, I mean it!"

Despite the pain, I managed to pull myself up and crawl upstairs. It felt like the steps were moving. I clung to the banister.

In her hand, my mother held a copy of that morning's *Waterbury Republican,* the local paper that was delivered daily to our front door and to the homes of almost every other family in our town and surrounding area. "Read this," she ordered, shoving the paper in front of me. Her hand shook as she pointed to "The Common Pleas Court," a listing of arrests, charges, and dispositions taken from the police blotter. There in black and white was my name, Kenneth Steele, my parents' address, and the charges: lewd act, resisting arrest, disorderly conduct, breaking the peace.

My head reeled. What lewd act had I performed? Why was there no mention of drunkenness or an overdose of pills? Didn't "they" understand that I was sick—sick of the voices, sick of myself, sick of everything? Stop the world, I had *tried* to get off. Again I had failed.

The phone rang all day long with calls to my mother from friends and neighbors, some sympathetic, others just hoping to learn more of the gory details. When my father arrived home, he ordered me to step outside. He wanted to speak to me in the car. "Do you know," he said calmly, "that 'The Common Pleas Court' is the third most-read section of the newspaper? First comes sports, next the obituaries, and then this. You might as well be on page one." He said that he'd had to answer to many people that day, both those he supervised and the person to whom he reported. And someone at work had posted the column on the employees' bulletin board, with my entry circled in red. "It was an enormous mistake for me to allow you to come home," my father said, looking straight ahead of him. He reminded me that Joey's friends and their parents were sure to know the news. "Once the charges against you are resolved," said my father evenly, "I expect you to leave here and never return."

My day in court arrived soon. I was represented by a legal aid attorney. He told me the allegation: that I'd exposed myself to another person in the bathroom at the train station. I found the very idea appalling. I had no memory of this act and have no history of doing this at any other time in my life. It goes against the very core of me. Even when I lived on the street, I made a great effort to assure that I was out of sight whenever I had to relieve myself outdoors. The attorney was surprised to hear from me about the pills and drinking and the fact that I was in some sort of unconscious state when the things I was charged with doing were alleged to have occurred, and he said he would speak to the bartender. He addressed the court, and the judge granted us a continuation of the case. In the meantime, bail was continued, and I returned to my parents' home.

My final paycheck was just enough to pay for some badly needed dental work. Two more teeth were pulled, and the dentist placed a temporary cap on another. I wouldn't have won any beauty contest, but at least I was free of the throbbing pain I had lived with since the assault. I was not, however, free of my fears for my future. The experience of having been placed in a "drawer" at Pueblo State Hospital would not leave me, and I felt abject terror at the possibility of being put in prison. In addition, I now also lived in mortal fear of the police. I knew what they could do to me. And I felt even more distance from my parents, who were counting the days to my departure. Joey kept more and more to his room when I was around. There was no one I could talk to, no one to help me manage my inner turmoil . . . and no medicine that could serve as a buffer between me and my infernal voices, which tormented me day and night. While they had claimed I was a loser before, they now owned written evidence that this was so. *You finally made the papers, Kenny, . . . not as a writer, but as a criminal,* they said. *Lewd act . . . disorderly conduct. Pig! Fucking pig! You're an animal, Kenny. We don't know if even hell will accept you now.*

They went on and on, and I became more and more desperate—so desperate that I then *knowingly* committed a criminal act. Worse yet, the people I hurt most were those responsible for bringing me into this world. I stole a check from my father's checkbook, made it out in the amount of $250, forged his signature, and cashed it at the bank where I had cashed my paychecks. Then I returned home, packed my belongings, and, carrying my two suitcases, sneaked out the back way of our house to Route 68 at the end of our street. I had in mind to head north toward Maine.

The day was as dark as my heart and wet as my tears. Rain mixed with ice, and I think the driver who picked me up would have taken pity on any stray cat out in that weather. He said he was heading to Hartford. Fine with me, I said. In a little while, he decided that this was not a good night for driving. We stopped in a small town, where I paid for a room of my own at a cheap motel.

I was stunned by dismay over what I had done. Alone that night (but for the voices), I got out notebook and pen and wrote a long letter to my father and mother, trying to explain why I'd left without having resolved the mess with the police. I promised to pay them back for the bad check (and I did, years later). Then I wrote to the attorney and judge, informing them that I'd left town without the knowledge or consent of my parents. I wanted to write to Joey but could not find the words. What do you tell your kid brother—that you love him? that you're sorry? that you hope his team wins? that he's better off without you in his life? I enclosed the correspondence to the lawyer and the judge in the envelope with the letter to my parents and addressed it to their home. The next morning, I bought a thirteen-cent stamp from the operator of the motel. He promised to mail the letter for me, and I took him at his word.

Dropped off in Hartford, I headed straight for a bar but, after one drink, decided that it was time to check out another hospital, another emergency room, another psychiatrist. I was hurting physically and emotionally. Soon I was in an ambulance, heading to Norwich State Hospital in the southeastern part of Connecticut, where I stayed for almost two years. One of the first things that happened there was that I was provided with a dental bridge and good dental care, for which I was very grateful. My body healed slowly. Little else distinguished this stay from many other institutionalizations. I now had the hospital routine down pat: Give us trouble and you'll regret it; behave well and you'll be rewarded. I was not about to cause more grief.

In time, I entered yet another halfway house and found another job in a nursing home as an orderly. I worked hard at my job, squirreling my salary away in a passbook account. I even cut down on my smoking (a habit I'd developed over the years in institutions), going from three packs a day to one to save the difference in cost. My new goal—inaugurated by the voices—was to earn enough to pay for a bus ticket from Connecticut to San Francisco, with some money left over for food and lodging when I got there. The reserve wouldn't have to last very long. I intended to make the ultimate suicide leap off the Golden Gate Bridge.

The bus ride to San Francisco took four days. My fellow travelers were a varied lot: elderly women who loved to tell their stories and understood that I would be a patient listener; family groups (mostly women with small children); male loners whom I knew to avoid. My years on the street had given me some intuitive skills that I put to good use.

I was paranoid during the entire trip. Concerned that "people" would do me harm and thwart my game plan, I kept my money hidden in my socks and tied my sneakers tightly, retrieving a ten- or twenty-dollar bill, as needed, in the privacy of a locked stall in the men's room of any rest area we visited. I had bought some paperback books before boarding the bus, and I read to lower the voices' volume. I also took Trilafon, the antipsychotic drug supplied me by the hospital upon discharge.

Through Utah, Nevada, then on to Sacramento . . . By the latter part of the journey, I had exhausted both my reading matter and medication, and the voices became raucous fellow travelers. I marveled that the other riders seemed not at all disturbed by them—or by me, for that matter.

Driving into San Francisco, with its rolling hills and deep blue bay spanned by a majestic bridge, was like entering Emerald City. It was a clear morning and the world seemed to sparkle. The bridge I had come to jump from wasn't gold at all but painted red. Still, I didn't feel cheated. San Francisco was to become my second favorite place anywhere, right after Manhattan.

Bus stations often are located in neighborhoods where low-cost lodging can be found. In San Francisco, that district is known as the Tenderloin. I stored my suitcases in a locker and went out looking for a hotel or rooming house that I could afford. I walked and walked the Tenderloin, checking out places that seemed more like flophouses than anything else. There had to be something better.

Carrying a copy of the *San Francisco Chronicle*, I entered a coffee shop near Market and Powell Streets, took a seat at the counter, ordered a cup of coffee, and sat drinking it while I skimmed the "Rooms to Let" section of the classifieds. There were several affordable listings on the fringe of the Tenderloin. The counterman directed me to Polk Street, where I soon found a weekly rental (toilet and bath down the hall) that seemed better than anything I had seen earlier. I took it, redeemed my luggage from the station, and moved right in.

First thing on my schedule was getting clean. After luxuriating in the shower for about a half hour, I emerged to find two guys waiting impatiently in the narrow hallway outside the bathroom. They let me know they were miffed. I gave them my Pueblo Hospital glare-and-growl routine, and they fell silent. Weighing about 210 pounds by now, I made an impression that was both imposing and intimidating. I figured I would lose some of that weight in the coming days by walking the streets in search of work.

The bad news, I quickly found out, was that I wouldn't be able to get a job as an orderly in a nursing home. California required special training and a certificate, which I didn't have. That left cooking as my primary skill, but I hadn't done any cooking in a long time and never had done quick grill work (a specialty area in which there seemed to be many jobs available). On the third day of my search, I ran into one of the two men who had waited outside the bathroom on my first day at the rooming house. I explained that it had been my first shower following a cross-country trip. The fellow, who was named Chuck, laughed and said it was okay; he understood. Would I like to join him for a cup of coffee?

At the counter of a nearby diner, I told Chuck that I was looking for a job and that I had some experience cooking in institutions. "Wait a minute," he said. "I may be able to help." As chance would have it, a friend from Chuck's hometown in Nebraska worked as a cook in a residence club in the area and, said Chuck, "I think he mentioned that he was looking for an assistant." He wrote down the friend's name (Rob), the name of the club, and the phone number. "Call and see if the position is still open," he suggested. "And use my name."

I phoned and made an appointment for the following day.

I located the club easily, met with Rob, and told him about my cooking experience in halfway houses and the nursing home in Westboro, Massachusetts. I was open about some of my psychiatric history, giving him an outline but not filling in all the details. He told me he liked my honesty and offered me a month's trial employment.

The residence club was a genteel sort of place that housed sixty-four people, men and women of varying ages. There was a range of accommodation, from private rooms with or without baths to shared quarters for two. Breakfast and dinner were included in the fee. I would be expected to help Rob prepare and serve two meals six days a week, plus a brunch buffet on Sundays. "If things work out," he said, "we'll make the arrangement permanent, and you'll be expected to move into a room here." I moved in before the month was up.

Enough with your promises, Kenny, taunted my voices. *Your word isn't worth a thin dime. You came here to end your life, not try to start it over again.* They warned, *Remember how many people you have hurt so far. You don't want to hurt these good people, too, do you? You must stop your work of destruction and finally die. You know where the bridge is. Use it!*

The voices were right. I *had* become caught up in the friendliness and the hope that I saw in San Francisco. If there was a geographic cure for my illness, I allowed myself to think, surely this was the place where I would find peace. Rob, my boss, was supportive; the club's tenants were friendly and appreciative, and I tried my hardest to remain safe and sane—going so far as to see a psychiatrist so that he could prescribe Trilafon, the one medication that managed at times to reduce the intensity of my voices and hallucinations, even when I took it at low doses. And I did take it—no tonguing the pills this time around.

In November 1978, the year I turned thirty, two horrific events occurred that affected many of the good people of San Francisco. First came the incredible tragedy of Jonestown, a commune established in Guyana by the Reverend Jim Jones, formerly of San Francisco (as were many of his followers). On a trip to Guyana to look into the doings of the People's Temple (as Jones's community was called), California Congressman Leo J. Ryan and four people who accompanied him were shot and killed. More than 910 of Jones's followers were also found dead, victims of a mass suicide brought about by drinking grape Kool-Aid laced with potassium cyanide. *(You're such a loser that you couldn't manage the death of one measly person,* said my voices, *and here more than 900 people had the courage to kill themselves.)* Jones was found shot in the head (whether by his own hand or another's was not certain). Many of the people I knew in the area, including several of my coworkers, lost friends and family in Guyana. I shared in their grief.

Nine days later, on November 27, San Francisco Mayor George Moscone and Harvey Milk, the city's popular and first openly gay supervisor, were gunned down by a man named Dan White, a former city supervisor. The nation watched on television as Acting Mayor Dianne Feinstein, then president of the Board of Supervisors, announced their deaths. That night, I joined thousands of San Franciscans in a walk from Market and Castro Streets to City Hall. Many of the marchers carried candles. All were in mourning. The only sound heard was that of people walking. Then Joan Baez, the folksinger, sang "Amazing Grace" in her clear, sweet voice, and all around me people began to cry.

I had trouble dealing with the deep and mixed feelings that these events created within me. I didn't know how to process all of the grief and pain I saw in every direction—from friends of mine to total strangers. I was beginning to lose it. My voices instructed me to down my entire supply of Trilafon with an industrial-strength cleaner that would be as toxic as the cyanide had proven for the residents of Jonestown. *Do it now, right away,* they spurred me on. *Bottoms up.*

For the first time ever, I confided what I was going through to a friend. I told Rob that I planned to commit suicide and that the voices were pushing me to get it over with right away. He listened attentively, then said, "I think it's time we got you some help, Shannon."

"Please don't tell people what I just told you," I said. "Please tell them that I'm suffering from depression over the loss of my lover, Karl." The stigma connected with schizophrenia was so strong that I'd rather have been seen as lovelorn than loco.

"This stays between us," Rob promised. Then he asked someone on the staff to please keep an eye on things in the kitchen while he drove me to a nearby hospital. To my surprise, I was not placed in restraints and shipped to a state institution. Instead, I was taken to Pacific Presbyterian Hospital, a private hospital in San Francisco that had a number of state-funded beds set aside for indigent patients, where I was placed on a psychiatric unit.

The contrast between being treated at this private hospital and my previous experiences in state institutions was like the difference between staying in a four-star hotel and being assigned a bed in a homeless shelter. Although a resident in a private unit could be restrained and placed in a quiet room (as at a state hospital), here one was constantly monitored—not isolated and ignored. In the private hospital, I was given a complete medical checkup, something I never received during my many stays in state hospitals. Here, too, I was assigned a team of professionals: a psychiatrist, a psychiatrist-in-training (resident), a social worker, and a primary nurse. I was being treated by people who cared, and the difference was startling.

The doctors were far more respectful of the patients. I told them which medications produced bad side effects and which were safer and more effective. They listened. They put me on a low dose of Trilafon along with a tolerable dose of Thorazine, which had been overprescribed for me in state hospitals. Like Trilafon, Thorazine helped lessen the intensity of my voices, but the dosage had to be monitored so that it would not cause the feeling of jumping out of my skin, the need to keep constantly moving.

The most important part of this hospitalization for me was that I had visitors every day, sometimes twice a day. They brought me books. They brought their friendship, which helped to combat the maleficent messages of my voices. People actually cared about me and wanted me to get well. As a result, I was able to leave the hospital after only five weeks, and I had a room, job, coworkers, and friends to be discharged to. If they could care that much about me, I told myself, I could care enough to try to fight the voices and hallucinations.

I wanted to do something useful with my life. Dianne Feinstein was running for election as mayor of San Francisco. I decided to use some of my free time to volunteer in her campaign. I helped with mailings, made phone calls to voters to poll them on various issues, and passed out literature at supermarkets and other public places. It was my first involvement in the political process, and I felt empowered. My interest in the mayor and my small role in her campaign would be greatly exaggerated by me in later years, when my illness became marked by delusions of grandeur—a heightened sense of self-importance and power commonly experienced in schizophrenia. (It's what leads some sufferers to claim to be Jesus Christ or the Messiah or the president of the United States or Elvis Presley.) I told people that I *ran* Mayor Feinstein's campaign. I also told them I attended Phillips Exeter Academy, Harvard College, and Harvard graduate school, assuming the background of my late friend Karl. I said these things often; at times, I even believed they were true.

In the meantime, I kept my day job. One day, Rob was visited by a friend in full naval dress uniform—a handsome man with a head of black hair and startlingly blue eyes. "The fleet's in," he told Rob jubilantly, and asked if there was a vacancy at the residence.

"Sorry, we're full," Rob told him, "but please stay and have dinner as my guest." Then Rob turned to me. "Shannon, this is Petty Officer Lee Royster Jr.," he said, "known as Junior to his friends. Can you find a place for him at one of the tables?"

I showed him to a seat. People in the room began to point at him and whisper. "Is it . . . ?" "Could it be?" Junior was a dead ringer for Fred Grandy, who played Burt "Gopher" Smith on the long-running television series *The Love Boat*, and was constantly being mistaken for the actor.

Later in the meal, I checked to see that he had everything he needed. After all, he was Rob's friend. "Everything's fine," he told me, "except that I'm a stranger in this town and have no plans for this evening and no one to share it with. Care to join me for a drink after work?"

"Sure," I said. "There's the P.S. Restaurant & Bar right down the street. Rob and I can probably make it once we've cleared things away." But Rob had other plans that evening, so I went alone to meet Junior. I was interested in hearing about life in the navy: where he had traveled, what he had seen. I was looking for another good story, but what I got instead was a pass. Almost immediately, Junior asked me to go back with him to his hotel. *That* explained his interest in me. I was hurt and offended. "You have the wrong guy," I said. "I'm no ho." I got up and walked quickly out of the bar.

Yes you are, Kenny, said my voices as I headed down the street, trying to walk off my anger. *Yes you are a ho, and he spotted you right away. You're a ho on sight. Everyone knows about you. The satellites circling the earth are sending your image and all the details about your sordid, sick life to everyone around the world.* The voices laughed, as if to say, How stupid can you be? Did you actually think you could change? Did you think you could make a new life for yourself?

I passed another bar and went in to try to still the voices and the demeaning message that they played like a broken record. *Ho . . . Sordid . . . Sick . . . Everyone knows about you.* I drank myself into oblivion and experienced the second blackout of my life. After I came to and shamefacedly returned to the residence, Rob told me that he thought I had a problem with alcohol and urged me to attend a meeting of

Alcoholics Anonymous. A group met in a community house right in the neighborhood.

At my first meeting, called a Speakers Meeting, I sat rapt as I listened to a man not much older than I talk about his life journey. Like me, he had been homeless. Like me, he had been plagued by demons. *Wow,* I thought. *Maybe I'm a paranoid* alcoholic *and not a paranoid schizophrenic.* The possibility that I might have been misdiagnosed all these years gave me optimism. Alcoholics could get better and stay that way. Schizophrenia, according to what I'd read, was a lifetime affliction. (Forget that *my* demons had first visited me when I was fourteen and that I hadn't had a drink until I was in my twenties. This wasn't about rationality; it was about hope.)

I waited till the end of the meeting to have a word with the speaker, a man named Joe Brennan. He invited me to join him at a nearby luncheonette where many AA members congregated. Joe was a counselor at Acceptance House, a residential community for recovering alcoholics and substance abusers. Over coffee, I told him my life story and asked whether I might be alcoholic instead of schizophrenic. He listened and said he thought it was likely.

He told me a bit about the organization. There was much in the AA experience and recovery process that I found appealing. AA asked one to admit powerlessness before drink. Well, I *was* powerless, only my nemeses were my demon voices and delusions. AA's emphasis on a higher religious power and making amends with those whom you have hurt fit right in with my Roman Catholic beliefs and upbringing. Best of all, AA didn't believe in the taking of psychiatric medicines. According to its tenets, these medications were as mood altering and addictive as alcohol. Joe invited me to join, offering to act as my sponsor—a kind of mentor, he explained. He would help guide me safely through the twelve steps of AA to sobriety and recovery. I agreed to attend ninety AA meetings in the next ninety days—a basic requirement of membership.

At each meeting, I listened and learned. Eventually, I, too, rose to address the audience. "My name is K. Shannon Steele," I said. "I'm a paranoid alcoholic. I used to believe I was a paranoid schizophrenic, but now I know I am an alcoholic." And then I told my story, a mixture of truth and embellishment (I was not just an alcoholic, but a Harvard-educated alcoholic). I had the audience in tears.

Joe suggested that I move into Acceptance House. I was reluctant to leave my job at the residence house, but I'd been experiencing some friction there. Rob and others who truly cared for me argued that my primary problem was not alcoholism; I desperately needed to believe that it was. And so I left job and friends and moved into Acceptance House, where Joe had promised me a job as house cook. He proved not to be as good as his word. What Joe wanted, it turned out, was to have me under his roof. What had happened to my street smarts? How could I not have seen this coming? I felt not just deceived, but terribly, incredibly stupid. Too stupid to live.

The voices directed me to another building, another rooftop from which I pondered whether and how to end it all. Then God sent another angel. Someone spotted me, phoned the police, and, as before, I was taken away in four-point restraints, this time to Napa Valley State Hospital, a place that rivaled Pueblo State in its inhumane treatment of the mentally ill. I was heavily sedated and placed in a glass-enclosed space that housed those psychiatric patients who required the most intensive care. The howls of my fellow inmates surrounded me like those of dangerous creatures lurking in a darkened beyond, except that I was in a fog and could not make them out. I knew only that I must be wary. When I gained consciousness and was released to the general psychiatric population, the situation was not much better. I drooled and barked with the best of them. It kept predators at bay.

In desperation, I placed a call to Rob. My reluctance to tell him just how stupid I had been was overcome by the strength of my desire to get out of this snake pit. Rob's response was warm and more generous than I deserved. He never said, "I told you so," never demanded more details than I was willing to provide. He told me that he was glad to get my call, that everyone had been worried about me, that he'd do his best to get me out, and that I still had a room and a job. I sobbed when I got off the phone. I cried even more a week later when I was back in my bed at the residence. I was grateful to be home.

There was a message for me to call the office of Lee Dolson, a member of San Francisco's Board of Supervisors. I waited several days before making the call. In my paranoia, I feared that it was a ruse, something that would get me recommitted to the wards at Napa Valley. When I phoned, a secretary answered and said yes, the supervisor wished to meet with me, then asked when would be a convenient time for me to come in. Despite the warnings of my voices—*The government's after you, Kenny; you've gone too far this time*—I agreed to meet with the supervisor at City Hall.

On the appointed day and time, Supervisor Dolson welcomed me into his office. He was a man of medium height, slightly paunchy, who could have been in his fifties or sixties. He showed me to a seat and moved to the chair behind a desk covered with mementos of his former career as a commander in the navy. He asked me to tell him something about myself. The story I told was that I had attended Exeter and received both bachelor's and master of business degrees from Harvard, that I'd had problems with alcoholism, and that I was now living in a residence in the area, trying to get my life back on track.

"I asked you here today on the recommendation of one of my advisers, a member of AA, who heard you speak at a meeting and recommended that I consider you for appointment to the Citywide Alcoholism Advisory Board," he said. "Unlike many other boards and commissions, the CAAB has real power. Members make the funding and licensing decisions." He leaned forward. "My adviser was right about you. Can I put your name forward for membership on the board?" I said yes, having no clue about what would be expected of me or whether I'd be up to the task.

The Supervisors Rules Committee, chaired by Board President John Molinari, confirmed the appointment of K. Shannon Steele without objection, and I soon found myself sitting on a board that approved, revised, or denied annual budgets for alcoholism and substance abuse programs. Early on, I was outraged when I saw how much money the county gave to the Salvation Army. In my experience, I told the board, the Army used its clients in recovery as unpaid labor. The organization had not been helpful when I'd turned to it, as a homeless man, for clothing or other assistance. I spoke passionately enough to have the CAAB chairman order an investigation into the Army's practices. When Acceptance House's budget came up for consideration, I asked the board to look at what I had discerned as a pattern of discrimination against admitting older men to the program. As a result of my involvement, I received a coveted Certificate of Honor for service to the community. Instead of enhancing my self-esteem, the acknowledgment only increased my feelings of worthlessness.

Shannon got the certificate, not you, said my voices. *What do you think the fine folks who honored Shannon would say if they knew that you're a fraud? What army would you turn to for salvation then? And who in the world would rescue you?* The more my achievement, the greater my apprehension that I'd be shown for who I really was: a high school dropout; graduate not of Harvard, but of innumerable hospitals and halfway houses; and an incurable *schizophrenic.* Daily, I lived in dread of being discovered and publicly dishonored.

My fears were so great that I resigned from the CAAB without explanation. I also left the residence, where I had been promoted to head cook following Rob's departure to open a similar residence club for international students. I couldn't handle the added responsibility for many reasons, including that my voices were rampant and that there was no longer anyone around in whom I felt it was safe to confide. Rob was gone and I was the boss. They needed me to be in charge, but I was falling apart. Once again, I hit the streets because the anguish of staying was too great. I yearned for the anonymity of homelessness and found it back in the Tenderloin district, where I prayed that someone—more crazed than I—would fatally attack me. *(Please, God, I* prayed, *let someone else do it. Let there be an end to my wretched life.)*

At the same time, I felt a paranoid fear of being recognized by some of the prominent citizens alongside whom I had recently worked. I decided to change my appearance and visited a hairstyling school in the district, where I asked them to make me a blond. (What they did, more accurately, was turn my hair yellow—the bright color of yarn stitched atop a rag doll. I will never forget the scalp pain caused by sitting under terribly hot lights for hours with chemicals in my hair.) The supervisors would not have recognized me. My own mother would not have known me in this guise. She wouldn't have wanted to.

For the next few weeks, I slept in doorways and parks. I took occasional meals in a soup kitchen run by the Glide Memorial Church, whose spiritual leader, the Reverend Cecil Williams, was as gracious to this dirty, homeless man as to the many important people who regularly turned to him for guidance. (In fact, the reverend and I had met briefly when I served as a member of the advisory board, but that was before I hit the streets and before I had this mop of strange hair.) He looked me in the eyes and he treated me well, finding me small chores to do around the church in exchange for shelter and an occasional payment.

I sank lower still. My home was an alley shared with two to three other men and hundreds of imagined creatures, theirs and mine. One evening, a short, thin man with big round eyes intruded into the space that I occupied. "What do you think you're doing here?" he said, as if he had a right to be here but I did not. "The police are rounding up street people tonight. Do you want to go to jail?"

I had never had my space so violated by anyone, not even by other homeless men. I was addled and angry. "Who do you think you are—Jesus Christ?" I growled.

"Nope," he said, extending his hand. "Steve Goldfinger. I'm a doctor who can put you in a hospital where you can get things sorted out. If nothing else, you'll have a bed and a few hot meals for a couple of days."

"Medicine, too?" I asked, for I knew well what happened in hospitals.

"Yeah, but I won't turn you into a vegetable," he answered, understanding the reason for my concern.

"I'm known here," I whispered conspiratorially. "If I agree to go with you, I need your promise that no one will be called."

"I promise that everything will be confidential," he said. "Will you let me admit you voluntarily?"

This was my first meeting with Stephen Mark Goldfinger, M.D., whom I now count as one of my friends and allies in the effort to gain better services and respect for people suffering from mental illness. In 1981, when we met, he was employed as the mental health director of the San Francisco Health Care for the Homeless, which was attached to San Francisco General Hospital. He's now a professor and vice chairman of the Department of Psychiatry at the State University of New York. He says he doesn't recall our first meeting. I know I'll never forget it.

Dr. Goldfinger had me admitted to General Hospital's psychiatric unit, a locked facility. The scene was a familiar one: patients overmedicated on Thorazine, Stelazine, and Haldol, shuffling back and forth like zombies in a dance of the bizarre. The carpeting, which reeked of tobacco, was covered with holes and burns caused by years of cigarettes being ground into the fibers. Immediately on entering, I was accosted by the strangest of couples: a little person playing an accordion and a tall man with badly bleached hair (I should know) playing hand clickers.

"You stay away from our audience," yelled the little person.

"You smell so bad, you could scatter a bunch of hungry pigeons and force them to fly away from a park where visitors were feeding them bread crumbs," shouted his tall friend.

I shook my head as if to clear it of hallucinatory images, but the duo was real. They weren't wrong, either. I didn't simply smell, I stank.

San Francisco General cleaned me up, put me back on Trilafon, and released me to Northeast Lodge, a supervised, locked residence with a day treatment program that offered structured activities intended to help patients make the transition from hospital to community. The idea was fine, but the curriculum offered no challenge to anyone past the age of five. My other option was to enroll in a program conducted in Spanish. I doubt that it had more relevance to real-life situations.

The Lodge was big on getting us out into the community, mandating attendance at museums, movies, and parks, either escorted or (once we were deemed responsible) in pairs or on our own. My roommate was the tall blond man who worked with the accordionist. He was actually a nice guy, and we would hang out together sometimes. One afternoon when I was granted a two-hour pass, I went to Fisherman's Wharf to see him and his partner perform. The little man also played the harmonica and flute, while my blond friend clicked his castanets and passed around a hat. The act was great.

There were other means of earning money, the partners soon taught me. One had to do with the testing of urine. Patients returning from off-campus outings were mandated to provide urine samples to be tested for drugs. Of course, many patients requested passes just so they could go out and get high. The musicians' advice was to sell the users my drug-free urine, which they'd then pass off as their own. My blond roommate was my very first customer. He was doing cocaine. By the time I left Northeast Lodge, I had twelve urine clients. But Sandy, a resident of the women's floor, had an even more thriving business among both women and men until the day that a routine urine check of male residents turned up several who were pregnant. Sandy hadn't known till then—nor had the administration—that she was in her fourth month.

For no clear reason, except that I was bored and was being prodded to get on with my death, I eloped from the Lodge during one of our recreational trips, this one to Land's End, a popular area with awesome cliffs that looked out at the Pacific Ocean and down at sandy beaches tucked into secret coves. I made my way to Route 1, a dangerous route on which to hitchhike because of its many curves. A driver swerving around a bend could easily miss seeing a pedestrian. *If that happens, so be it,* I thought.

Instead, I was picked up by two guys in a Jeep, who drove first to Los Angeles, then on to Palm Springs. I went with them. Along the way, they talked of the dangers of the high desert. They said there were rattlesnakes and scorpions. Coyotes, running in packs, had recently been reported attacking children and some adults in the area. This was it: a new way to die. As soon as we reached Palm Springs, I headed for the high desert, where I came closest to having my death wish fulfilled. A rattlesnake, sunning itself on a rock, blended in so well with its environment that I practically sat on it. Startled by my action, the snake moved with lightning speed, biting me twice—once in my backside and the second bite in my lower calf. Then it moved on.

My voices cheered. *Kenny's dying, Kenny's dying, Kenny's dying. It's over, over, over . . . and we've won.*

The sun beat down on me. In my mind's eye, I saw myself lying on the rock where I'd been bitten when another rattler, seven to eight feet in length, slithered over to me, then spoke to me directly. *I'm your Moby Dick rattler,* he said, *and you are my Ahab. You have been seeking me ever since the voices first told you to kill yourself. It was my fate to do the deed for you. I now have to find and devour the rattler who poisoned you so that he doesn't boast of his victory to the demons. He's not the one to take credit. Your death belongs to me.*

The Moby Dick rattler took a big bite out of my jugular vein, and a river of blood ran thick and swift from my neck. *Just so there won't be any doubt about who's the victor,* said the snake, *I'll carry your head with my jaw prints in it to the demons so that I can claim my bounty. But that comes later. For now, I have ordered a band of coyotes to watch over you while I go to devour that other rattler.* I looked around. Three fierce, snarling, salivating coyotes stood over me. Moving off, the huge snake glanced back to where I lay and said, *You could say "Thank you," you know. Your misery on earth ends here. Now you, too, can become a demon voice. You can guide others the way your demons have been guiding you.*

"Mr. Steele!" I ignored the woman's voice calling my name. "Mr. Steele!" It was even more demanding. I shut my eyes so tight, I thought my eyeballs would pop out of their sockets. "Mr. Steele!" This time, the voice was accompanied by a firm touch; the speaker was shaking me. If I were dead, could I feel her touch? Was this another hallucination? Did the voice belong to an animal disguised as a woman? If a delusion, what did this she-devil want with me? If real . . . if I was still alive, did I want to come back and be faced with my ever-present voices, my lifelong companions, my hell on earth?

I opened my eyes and saw a nurse and doctor standing over me. "Well, Mr. Steele, you just made it," said the doctor. "You were bitten three times by a rattler." I wondered if the third bite was by Moby Dick. "No," said the doctor, when I asked about the jugular vein. "If you'd been bitten there, it would have meant instant death." He told me that I'd also been bitten by a coyote that was being tracked by several hunters. They were the ones who found me lying on the rock, still breathing.

"Good thing it was some good ol' boys who knew what they were doing," said the doctor. "They did all the right things and got you here to Desert Hospital as quick as a jackrabbit. You can thank those men and the good Lord for being alive."

You can curse those men, said my voices. *Damn those men, damn the doctor, damn everybody to hell.* The voices were furious.

I looked past the glass pane of the door to my hospital room and saw a security guard. "What's he here for?"

"Well, Mr. Steele," said the doctor, introducing himself, "I'm Dr. Winslow and I'm a psychiatrist. You expressed a lot of suicidal thoughts when you were delirious with fever. You also told the men who found you that you wanted to die and asked them to leave you to the vultures. The guard is there to see that you don't do harm to yourself. I've committed you to observation at Loma Linda Medical Center. They have a first-rate psychiatric unit. I think you will thank me for this someday."

"Thank you? Who are you to interfere?" I shouted at the man. "Get out and don't come back!"

I was placed in four-point leather restraints that held me firm to the hospital bed. The next morning, the ambulance drivers removed me to a gurney, and, still restrained, I was taken to Loma Linda, a teaching hospital run by Seventh-Day Adventists. MediCal, California's version of Medicaid, was paying for my stay. While here, I received a permanent MediCal card, essential for an indigent person to access needed services in this state.

I began my stay in seclusion, with the door open and a one-to-one suicide staff member assigned to me. Soon I was free to walk about the unit, a clean, pleasant area with lots of room to roam. My aide stayed with me. Just as the hospitals had their routines, so did I. I fell silent—speaking to no one, not the admissions clerk, not the medical resident who introduced himself to me, not the other patients. It was my normal way of responding to abnormal feelings of deepest depression: case the joint and say nothing. Had the staff not been provided with my records from Desert Hospital, they could well have thought I was mute. I refused food and lost thirty pounds in three and a half weeks. I refused to let any medicine pass my lips. At night, however, they restrained me to my bed and fed me intravenously. I didn't know that they added medication to the feedings. Ultimately, the doctors told me, they had no choice but to move on to electroconvulsive therapy (a drastic procedure I wanted to avoid) since psychoactive-drug therapy had failed to be effective in my case. I ignored their words but not those of the voices.

Do it, do it, do it, they chanted. *Get electrocuted! Do it this time before it's too late!* Then I heard the commanding voice of The Ruler: *Do it or the pains you will suffer on the streets and in the hospitals will be so horrid, you'll be praying for the chance to be shocked out of existence.* His was the voice that brought me close to the edge.

I underwent nine shock treatments. I was talking and eating again. I had little memory of recent events and the roles that people had played in them. The voices returned immediately—they'd never really left—proving ECT's ineffectiveness in treating the type of paranoia and command hallucinations I was experiencing. Command hallucinations are auditory instructions that tell people to act in a certain way. These instructions can range from the trivial—*Wear a red shirt*—to demands to commit a harmful act. Over half of command hallucinations are to commit suicide, which my voices constantly egged me on to do. In some few cases (but never in my own experience), the person receives instructions to hurt others.

My depression did lift, however, and I stopped thinking of suicide all the time.

Loma Linda discharged me to an L facility—*L* being short for *long-term stay*. The site was a former nursing home. We men lived two, three, and four to a room in an environment that made me look back on some of the public shelters I had been in as the Ritz. I escaped from here to be picked up and placed in yet another hospital. Back and forth I went until a final hospitalization, in San Diego, where my MediCal coverage ran out, and I no longer had to escape, for I was discharged to the streets.

I located a dark, narrow bar on a side alley and went in, hoping to find some chips or nuts in a dish on the counter. Frequently, I could find someone to buy me a drink. If I struck it lucky, I might get a burger and fries. I looked over the clientele and spotted someone who seemed familiar. Another delusion? The man looked up, smiled, and said, "Hi, Shannon. What are you doing here?" It was Junior. He wasn't in uniform and he was tying on one hell of a drunk, but you would still mistake him for "Gopher." I needed sleep and a shower more than food and drink, so I asked if he had a place where I could stay for a night or two. "Sure," he said. He would have said sure or nope or anything anybody wanted, he was that drunk.

I helped him to his feet, and we took a cab to a private house in El Cajon, California, just outside of San Diego. I figured that this was his home away from the naval base. I got him to bed, then I showered and crashed on the sofa, where I slept until midafternoon of the next day. Junior was gone when I awoke, but he'd left me a note saying that he'd return at six. That evening, when he came home from work, I learned what he now did during the day. Junior had been discharged from the service and was employed as a sanitation worker for the Port of San Diego.

I spent a couple of weeks with Junior, but he wasn't Karl. I didn't care enough to help him from one binge to another. I felt a need to move on and told him so. "Ever been to Hawaii?" he asked. I hadn't and agreed to go with him. After two days on Oahu at the Royal Hawaiian Hotel, I decided that I'd had enough. I couldn't deal with Junior's embarrassing conduct in public and his demands on me in private. I walked out on him and went out onto the streets of Waikiki. There was a rainbow in the sky, but I wasn't interested in finding the pot of gold that's proverbially at its end; what I wanted was Valium and booze. I had fifty dollars in my pocket, enough to pay for both . . . and bring on another blackout.

I awoke in a strange bed. Somebody had brought me to his home. This time, my body worked out my escape. I experienced some kind of medical event, very much like a heart attack, and was rushed to Castle Hospital in Kaneohe, Hawaii, on the other side of the Pali Highway that separates Waikiki from Kaneohe. The diagnosis was a major asthmatic attack, but my erratic behavior was such that a psychiatric consult had been ordered, which then led to my being transferred to the hospital's psychiatric unit. By this time, I could write a book: *The Schizophrenic's Coast-to-Coast Guide to Psychiatric Institutions and Halfway Houses*. As I improved (I never recovered; I just was able at times to better control my behavior), I once again became a candidate for a halfway house and was accepted by one called The House, at the top of Sierra Drive in Honolulu, with an incredible view of Diamond Head, downtown Waikiki, and rainbows that spanned the horizon each and every day. I lived in Hawaii for three years, a period in which I was even less able to manage my disease because my physical health seriously deteriorated.

Since the asthma attack, I was put on prednisone and took a daily dose for almost two years. My face blew up to the point where I had to search for my neck; I looked like a chipmunk. There was oxygen and a nebulizer at the ready in my room, in case I experienced trouble breathing. The prednisone made me manic. It also made me gain weight. I shot up from 230 to 400 pounds and was in and out of Queens Medical Center with pneumonia. I was too sick, too old (in my mid-thirties, I felt aged as Methuselah), and had too many medical problems to look for a job as a cook, orderly, or anything else. I was hanging around The House all day, which wasn't acceptable to the administration. They told me to find something to occupy my time.

And so one day I went down to the Diamond Head Mental Health Center and asked if there was anything I could do. I thought I might put in some hours as a receptionist or do something else, like address envelopes, where I'd be able to sit at a desk. After I'd been volunteering at the center's Office of Community Support for a short time, the social worker came up to me. "I want to start some self-help groups that are culturally sensitive to the various groups in the area," she said. At about this time, Hawaii had very few peer-run programs. "How would you like to do some research on what's available on the mainland?" It sounded interesting.

She told me how to do a literature review and had me look into AA programs and other peer-directed groups. It started out as a small effort. I think the center's staff knew that I liked to read and thought that, in looking at self-help for others, I might begin to help myself. The more I read, the more I began to think about what might be helpful for *mental health consumers* like me. This was a new term and a new concept that made sense. People like me weren't just patients to be acted upon by a paternal health care establishment, I realized; we were consumers of health care services. As such, we had a right to be included in plans for our own treatment; we had a right to have a say in the system that was charged with seeing to our welfare. Who, after all, cared more than we did? My experience as a member of the alcoholism advisory board had shown me that consumer participation in programs could make a difference. But mental illness is not like addiction. Turning yourself over to a higher power isn't going to take away your illness. We needed something different.

I ended up writing a pretty nice paper. I also started a group at The House called *Ho'omaka Hou* (for New Beginnings) for people to come together, share their stories and concerns, and find direction for their lives. (Ironically, it proved not to be a new beginning for me.) I then found out there were similar self-help groups (with names like Recovery, Inc.) in other communities in Hawaii and felt that one umbrella organization could coordinate the several efforts and be more successful in effecting change. Someone told me that I ought to write a grant and present it to the Hawaii house and senate. I did, and with the help of the social worker and others who looked over the outline and made suggestions, we won major legislative funding ($60,000), plus office space for the initiative, called the Office of United Self-Help, which still exists.

All this activism brought me to the attention of Governor George Ariyoshi, who appointed me as the first mental health consumer to serve on the State Council on Mental Health. In July 1984, he also sent me, as Hawaii's representative, to the first Alternatives Conference for Mental Health Consumers, Recipients, Survivors, and Ex-patients, held in Baltimore, Maryland. Of course, my voices accompanied me.

What no one who saw or dealt with me during this period knew was that my voices had been out of control all along and that I'd continued to live in an increasingly delusional world. I was still K. Shannon Steele, still a graduate of Harvard, still someone who'd served as primary adviser to Dianne Feinstein. Along the way, I added a few more trophies to my shelf. I never told my own psychiatrist or anyone associated with me about who I really was or what my real illness was all about. I continued to say that I was an orphan, continued to insist that I suffered from depression over the loss of a lover, continued to deny the severity and reality of my schizophrenia. A part of me believed everything I told others: In my heart of hearts, Dianne Feinstein *was* my good friend; Harvard *was* a great school, but not as difficult as people assumed. This public me could get up and speak and move others to action, while the private me cowered from the voices that knew and proclaimed the truth: *Why stop at Dianne Feinstein?* they taunted me. *Why not claim you're a good friend of President Reagan? That Nancy has had you to tea? Liar, liar,* they shouted. *The world will find you out.*

The burden of it all, illness *and* guilt, proved too much. The better known I became, the worse were my fears of being discovered. Moving on made no sense, but I wasn't being governed by sense. I knew only that I had to get as far away from Hawaii as possible—and that meant New York. And so I flew back to familiar territory and a well-worn script. Once again, I walked the streets of the city, sleeping on park benches or in any space that could accommodate me.

Again I got myself up to the top of a tall building and tried to end my life by jumping off, as if all that had gone on in the intervening years counted for nothing.

In the late 1980s, I was back where I began, in a psychiatric hospital on Wards Island.

And I paced the floor.

{ 7 }

Second Chances

MANHATTAN STATE HOSPITAL, on Wards Island, had been renamed Manhattan Psychiatric Center in the early 1970s to make clearer its mission: the treatment of people with mental illness. Although I plainly fit the category, I'd found it hard to gain entrance to the hospital this time around because New York State had been systematically cutting the number of beds available to mental patients. And so I spent eight weeks under close observation on one of Roosevelt Hospital's Psychiatric Tower units. There I underwent one "utilization review" after another to demonstrate that I remained a danger to myself. Had it not been for the chief psychiatric resident's tenacious efforts to hold me on the unit at Roosevelt until a place at Manhattan Psychiatric became available, I would have been sent out to the streets weeks earlier, left to fend for myself in a world filled with danger.

Others were not so lucky. Increasingly, psychiatric patients (many dangerous to themselves or to others) were being discharged when their Medicaid coverage ran out after only three or four weeks' treatment. They were handed a ten-day supply of medication and a list of public shelters, which even the mad knew to be hostile places. Settling in stairwells and on sidewalks, this throwaway population drew attention only when it was seen as a public nuisance (like the squeegee men who swoop down on stopped cars to beg loose change of irritated drivers) or when some tragically crazed man or woman, off medication, made headlines by committing a violent act. And so I was grateful when Manhattan Psychiatric Center accepted me.

It didn't take long to see that more than the institution's name had changed since the last time I'd stayed here. Meyer 2-G, a locked unit in the new building to which I'd been assigned, was co-ed! My first concern, however, was keeping my pants up—and not because there were women on the ward. The hospital's clothing store held little that was large enough to fit me, and I became heir to two pairs of oversized pants and two shirts that had belonged to a patient even more obese than I. Because I'd been placed on suicide watch, I was not allowed to wear a belt or suspenders and had to walk around holding my pants up with both hands. *Look at what a fat pig you've become,* the voices derided me. *Fat pig has been taken to the slaughterhouse. Chop off his head!*

I was assigned to a room next to the nurses' station so I could be closely observed. I saw this as a vast improvement over being placed in four-point restraints and held in isolation. But other aspects of this incarceration, which lasted about a year and a half, were very troubling. For one thing, the staff not only sanctioned the ethnic tension among residents, but encouraged the resultant flare-ups; tabloid headlines about racial strife in the outside world became raging battles in the universe of Meyer 2-G.

I managed to stay out of most of these clashes. I have never mistrusted people because of the color of their skin. I became paranoid only when the voices would whisper, *Watch out for that fellow in the corner; he's got a knife in his hand* (when in fact he was raising his finger), or when they'd warn, *Be careful of that nurse; she's giving you poison* (and it was only medicine). The "higher" a ward would become (meaning the more dangerous it was), the greater were my efforts to step outside of my surroundings. Even when things were relatively calm, I felt as if I were communicating with people through a gauze barrier that separated me and my voices from the real world. When things grew tense, I'd simply lower that curtain and retreat into books (whenever possible) in an effort to keep the voices at bay. But the hospital staff had a different objective, I soon learned. Many were dedicated to keeping us hospitalized as a means of retaining their jobs.

"Generations of my family have worked here," I overheard a gray-haired senior aide tell two young staff members, "and now my own son can't be hired unless someone retires, goes on disability, or dies." She went on to explain that there was a movement, in New York and elsewhere, to close state hospitals and send "these crazies" back into the community. "If they are here, we need to keep them here," she said definitively.

She was talking about acute psychiatric cases (like many patients on our unit) as well as the "chronic" and "refractory" types who'd been banished to the back wards of Dunlap, the neighboring building. It is the disease of schizophrenia—not the afflicted people—that is refractory, meaning that it is resistant to treatment. These frequent put-downs, often said within patients' hearing, were capable of destroying any vestige of self-worth that any of us had managed to hold on to. At one time or another, in one or another mental institution, I had been tagged with these labels. They made me lose hope that I could ever be cured of my illness or relieved of its symptoms.

I settled back into institutional life, where the constant activity of my voices (sometimes loud, more often chattering away in the background) was even welcome, because it served as a minor distraction from the boredom, the mind-numbing monotony of day-to-day existence on the ward. From 6:00 A.M., when we were awakened, until 6:00 P.M. (showers and bed), there was little for us patients to do but play cards, chess, or checkers, fantasize, find something from a meager store of books to read (for some reason, every hospital had a copy of William Shirer's *The Rise and Fall of the Third Reich;* I must have read it five or six times from cover to cover), pace the floors, or watch television. Another notable change on this ward was that the TV wasn't going all the time but was placed in a separate room where those who wanted to watch could do so, and others like me could keep their distance. On Saturday mornings, a program called *Soul Train,* featuring favored rap and pop music artists, played to a standing-room-only crowd.

For those without off-ward privileges, the major events of the day were mealtimes: breakfast at 7:00, lunch at 11:00, and dinner at 4:00. We'd line up long before the dining room opened, even though the food was notoriously bad: steamed, overcooked, and all but inedible. Waiting in the hallway, with my security guard at my side, I could smell corned beef and cabbage long before I saw what was being served, and I drooled—in reaction to the medication, not in anticipation of the meal. The corned beef tasted like no meat ever found in home or restaurant; the cabbage was like paper. I could not eat it. If either lunch or dinner was delayed, however, a sense of agitation would take over the unit. People would start to pace—faster, faster, around and around in circles—because the routine had been altered.

Two or three times a day, as well, we'd be expected to line up for meds. I was being given medical drugs plus a pill to lower my blood pressure and, I think, a diuretic, because I found myself going to the bathroom with great frequency. From time to time, the people dispensing medication would call out "Mouth inspection," and the patients would have to open wide. Woe to anyone caught "tonguing" pills—the medication would then be given in liquid form. Before I left the hospital, many patients were being injected with the antipsychotic medications Prolixin and Haldol. There was no way to tongue those.

Group therapy sessions were held several times a week. I'd shuffle over to where the group was sitting—eight or ten patients to a doctor—just because it was something to do. Then I'd sit there commenting, in conspiratorial fashion, on what others were saying.

"How did you feel about the visit from your family?" the doctor asked one of the women in the group.

"Well, I'm worried about my daughter," she replied.

Then *I* interjected, "Ha! *She* thinks that her children still remember her. . . ." People who knew me then tell me that I'd start giggling, making noises that were conversational in tone although not in content; I'd cover my mouth and begin whispering, in the same way that my voices whispered to me. This fed into the paranoia of the other patients: Why was I whispering about them? I was often asked to leave the group. But it mattered little to me if I stayed or left. We were all trapped in the same game. One never knew what anyone was going to say or do . . . or when somebody would break out in sobs or manic laughter.

The first patient to greet me soon after I arrived on this ward was Paul, a fellow in his early thirties who stood just my height and weighed half as much as I did. Actually, Paul didn't so much greet me as tell me his name and then slump into a chair next to mine, where he sat without uttering another word. A couple of hours later, he rose, said, "Been nice talking with you," and disappeared.

I was startled by both his coming and his going, for I had been preoccupied with my demons, actively listening to their endless chattering about the necessity of my death and the manner in which I could carry it out in this place. *Coward,* they called me. *Chicken,* they said. *You haven't the guts to kill yourself.* The voices divided themselves into choral sections. One group chanted, *Who's afraid to kill himself, kill himself, kill himself?* And the other responded, *It's fat Kenny.* For the first time in a long while, I found myself talking back to them. "Who are you calling a coward?" I shouted, my voice rising to the challenge. "Just dare to show me who you are and we'll see which of us is the stronger and braver." I'd taken Golden Gloves boxing as a young adolescent, and I jumped up (dropping my pants), assumed a fighting stance, and began throwing blows against an unseen enemy.

The next thing I knew, I was being punched in the face by a fellow patient, a big black man who believed that my words had been directed at him. "That's for Yusef," he shouted as he hit my nose with an uppercut. (Yusef Hawkins was a black youth who had recently been beaten to death by white guys in a neighborhood known as Bensonhurst, in Brooklyn.) The blow fractured my nose. I struggled to fight back, signaling the beginning of a free-for-all. The attendants—including one assigned to guard me on suicide watch—observed the melee and did nothing. More men joined the attack on me, and the noise level rose as the fighting continued.

At some point, someone must have given me an injection, for I woke in a padded seclusion room, lying on a bare, thin mattress. I sat up, startled, then dropped to the side, my head hitting the cold marble floor. It was not the first time this had happened. I believed that the sleep disruptions and falls I was experiencing were the work of my voices; they were trying to make me break my head open and die. The hospital staff decided that the falls were inept attempts at suicide, much like the cuts and scratches that some patients make on their wrists without severing an artery. As it turns out, we were both wrong.

To be on the safe side, the staff restrained me in bed each evening. Many a night I would wake up, gasping for breath and unable to move. It felt as if someone were sitting on top of my chest. As I struggled to sit up, I felt a burning sensation from the leather straps that held my wrists and ankles fast. The more I pulled on the straps, the tighter they became. I called out for help. "I can't breathe," I told the attendant who finally responded.

"It's all in your head," he replied, dismissing my complaint. (This was a common response to patients' reports of physical discomfort or pain, not just at Manhattan Psychiatric, but at other hospitals that housed the mentally ill.)

Nor did I fare any better with the attending medical residents, who wanted nothing more than to make it through this unwelcome rotation in their medical education and move on. As far as they were concerned, I could go on banging my head against the floor. And, night after night, that was just what I did.

What if I die? I wondered, for I had known patients to "disappear" during the night—never to be heard of again. Any questions about their whereabouts were met by silence from the staff. This ignorance of the fate of those who'd disappeared fed the patients' paranoia. I wanted to die, but I didn't want to just fade away—and my nightly struggles to breathe had me terrified into thinking that could happen. I had no visitors, no family to care what happened to me. One morning, as Paul and I waited on line for the powdered eggs that were that day's fare, I turned to him and hastily whispered, "Paul, I need a favor from you. If I'm not here one morning and just disappear, call the police and tell them there was a conspiracy by the staff to have me suffocate to death. Will you do that?"

Paul nodded solemnly. "I promise," he said.

Christmas and New Year's came and went with little fanfare on Meyer 2-G—and with no change in my situation. It was early 1990, and I was still being denied ground privileges, which meant that I was also prevented from applying for a job in one of the buildings on campus and earning the money that I needed to buy coffee and cigarettes. And so I turned to a trade I knew: selling my urine. Patients would use their ground privileges to leave the island via the bridge to 103rd Street, where eager entrepreneurs waited to sell them feel-good drugs and alcohol. After returning to the ward, these same day-trippers were required to undergo a urine check for substance abuse. My urine was certifiably drug free, and therefore a desirable purchase. I was paid five dollars a specimen.

In the spring, I was finally taken off suicide watch and granted permission to go outside. I found a paying job as an assistant in the medical library, located in Dunlap. Here I was surrounded by journals and books, and I learned how to use WordPerfect on the computer. At first, I found the keyboard confusing and would gaze for hours at a blank blue screen. But I was given a manual and practice time, and eventually I became proficient in the computer's use. I also learned how to create and maintain alpha and numeric filing systems. It was responsible work and much better than the mindless assembly-line work, like putting plastic dinnerware and napkins into see-through containers, that was usually offered hospital patients.

I spent many of my off-duty hours with Paul, who clung to me like a shadow. "I'm here on orders from John Gotti to keep an eye on the blacks," he whispered to me early on in our acquaintance. (Paul and I were two of the three white males on the ward.) "He sent you here to check up on me, didn't he?"

"John who?" I said. I had never heard of the man, but Paul filled me in on the exploits and power of the notorious underworld leader.

"I'm Gotti's right-hand man," he confided. "They're all scared of me around here."

I wasn't scared, and in all other respects Paul proved an amiable companion, guiding and encouraging me on my first foray into the city on a pass from the hospital. We saw a movie, *The Hunt for Red October,* and had pizza . . . just like normal people. Then we returned to Meyer and had our urine tested.

"My mom's coming to take me out to brunch this weekend," Paul told me one day. "Request a pass for Sunday so you can join us."

I hesitated. I didn't want to break in on family time; but Paul persisted, and so I agreed to join them "just this once," which quickly became every other Sunday. We would go to a restaurant on Manhattan's East Side that featured an all-you-can-eat buffet. Paul's mom treated me like a second son, even to the point of offering to provide me with a weekly allowance. I declined. I suffered many delusions over the years, especially believing that the world revolved around me, but I would not permit myself the deception of thinking that Paul and his mother were my family. The very notion of *family* caused me pain, for though I pretended to others that my mother and father were dead, I knew that I had real parents and a real brother living in Connecticut. I also knew that I was on my own.

Before I could be placed in a community rehabilitation and housing program, I needed to file an application for Supplemental Security Income (SSI). Coverage by this program would financially support the move to housing. This was an important first step toward leaving the hospital; without SSI, I would also not have the Medicaid coverage to pay for clinic visits, qualify for day treatment programs, or have prescriptions filled.

My many efforts to meet with the social worker who could help me were frustrated. Whenever I arrived at his office for a scheduled meeting, he wasn't there. Sorry, he'd tell me later. He was either away from his desk or on vacation. He kept changing appointments. Was this a plot? Along with my regular voices, the words of the gray-haired aide, *We need to keep the crazies here,* kept drumming in my ears. Is that what the social worker was trying to do—keep me there?

I complained to the head nurse of the unit. "The social worker won't see me," I said.

"I'll look into it," she promised.

Several weeks went by without any word, except from the new voice in my head: *If he's here . . .* Over and over again I heard it: *. . . we need to keep him here.*

Desperate, I asked one of the medical residents to investigate the situation. "I need to see a social worker," I said, "or I'll be doomed to live out my days in this place." The resident found the record of all the broken appointments and brought them to the attention of the chief psychiatrist. From then on, my social worker was in when I called! Together, he and I filled out and filed the requisite paperwork. Finally, I was able to move on to a rehabilitation program in the community.

Fountain House, the program to which I was assigned, is located on West Forty-seventh Street in the area of Manhattan known as Hell's Kitchen, where I'd previously lived. On my first visit, it looked a lot closer to heaven than hell. The entrance room was furnished with the kind of old sofas and chairs that give one the feeling of home; vases of fresh-cut flowers were placed about. A man came forward to greet me.

"Shannon Steele?" he asked, smiling and reaching out his hand to clasp mine in greeting. I nodded. "I'm Ronnie Peterson," he said. "Let me show you around the clubhouse, so you can decide on the area in which you want to volunteer."

Clubhouses are gathering places for people with serious and persistent mental illness, where they receive much-needed emotional support and some sort of vocational training. Working (for free) with staff at this well-endowed, non-profit organization was seen as part of the job of recovery.

Ronnie led me through a brief tour of several units: reception, orientation, clerical, education, maintenance, horticulture, kitchen, dining room, snack bar, housing, and administration. The idea of working with plants and flowers was appealing. I also felt an instant rapport with Bodil Drescher Anaya, the Danish-born horticultural therapist who ran the unit. The choice was easy.

The first several weeks, I continued to live at Manhattan Psychiatric Center, commuting an hour and a half to my volunteer job at Fountain House in the morning, then returning to the hospital, where I worked, afternoons, in the medical library—my sole source of much-needed income. *You'll never make it on the outside,* said my voices, who rode with me on the buses, stood beside me on the subway platform, waited with me at red lights and crossed with me on the green. *Wait and see. . . . You'll run again . . . and hide, but we'll find you,* they predicted. *Wherever you are, we will be there, too. We're the best friends you have, Kenny. Don't you know that by now? How much more will it take for you to realize that your destiny is to fail at everything except killing yourself?*

I worked in spite of my delusional voices and because of them: I was going to prove them wrong. One afternoon, I received a call at the medical library from someone at Fountain House. He asked if I'd be interested in a job in the mail room of the National Resource Defense Council (NRDC), at Fifth Avenue and Twentieth Street. This would be a "transitional employment" placement, meaning that Fountain House would supervise my performance. I accepted; it paid more than the library. What I didn't realize was that the job belonged to Fountain House, not to me. The distinction was to prove critical.

By everyone's assessment, I was ready to move out of Manhattan Psychiatric Center, but there were no appropriate vacancies in any of the residences managed by Fountain House. Instead, I was discharged to something called a three-quarter-way house on the grounds of Wards Island. Twenty-eight days was the maximum length of stay here. During that time, I was expected to get my housing and discharge plans organized and completed. I was also required to check into a state outpatient clinic, where I'd meet with a social worker and psychiatrist once a week and receive the Trilafon I was then taking.

The only hard part of moving out of Manhattan Psychiatric was leaving Paul behind. I had hoped he would join me at Fountain House, but he was afraid of leaving the place where he had spent most of his adolescence and (but for brief periods at home) all of his adult life. Like so many others, Paul had grown dependent on the mental health system to monitor his behavior and meet his everyday needs. It's an all-too-common scenario: The loss of self-esteem that accompanies mental illness leads to dependence on medicines, alcohol, doctors, intermittent hospitalizations, clubhouses, halfway houses, SSI . . . round about and back again. There is a dread of independence that makes a person return to the perceived safety of the system time and again. Lord knows, I have been there many a time. My friend Paul was never going to venture out.

I tried to explain to Paul that Fountain House was an extension of that system. "This clubhouse is just like a hospital," I told him on a sunny afternoon the day before I was to leave. "The whole idea of the place is to protect you as part of a core community where everyone lives, works, eats, and socializes together. You can depend on them." But Paul would have none of it, or of me, either. From that day on, he would not join me for a movie, would not meet me for a pizza, would even refuse to take my phone calls. The senior aide's words reverberated through my head: *We need to keep the crazies here.* She had won a victory with Paul.

As part of my job in the horticulture unit, I was assigned to a weekend at High Point Farm in Montague, New Jersey. Owned by Fountain House, this was a working farm with cattle, horses, pigs, chickens, and a large vegetable garden. Alec, who also volunteered in the horticulture unit, and I were to help plant the spring crop. This was my first meeting with Alec. In the evening, our chores done, we would sit together on the guest house patio, gaze out at the new-green lawn, at the giant trees coming back to life, at the expanse of starlit sky, and talk about our lives.

"I can't believe that I, a schizophrenic who lives on Wards Island, am sitting in this glorious place," I said. "If it's a delusion, I don't want any medication that will make it go away."

Alec laughed. "How do you get back and forth to work?" he asked.

I told him about the two buses, the train, the long walk from the station, followed, hours later, by the return trip. He said that he had his own apartment near Fountain House headquarters and invited me to stay over whenever I wanted.

After we returned to the city, I took him up on his offer. Alec's story bore many similarities to my own, including hearing voices and experiencing multiple hospitalizations. He liked tales filled with fantasy and introduced me to *Star Wars, Star Trek,* and *The Never-Ending Story.* Finally, Fountain House found a supportive apartment for me in a doorman building at West End Avenue and 102nd Street. The apartment was huge. I had three roommates; two had their own quarters, and I shared a room with the third. It wasn't a bad arrangement, but then Alec invited me to move into his place. He liked having me around, he said. It kept him from being alone with his voices.

The move was right for several reasons, mostly that Alec and I got along so well. I also liked the fact that it gave me some measure of independence. I wasn't comfortable with Fountain House being my day treatment program, my employer, and my landlord. I cut one string of dependency, and it felt good.

Then I tried to cut a few others. One day, I phoned the SSI office and asked them to cancel my application for benefits, the application I'd spent so much time completing. I didn't need to be part of a system, I said. I could work for my income. I told myself that I didn't need Medicaid or medications, either. Didn't I have two jobs, one apartment, a good friend? I could go to the movies when I wished, could read any book that I wanted. . . . When the voices were especially abusive or demanding (they still wanted my death), I often could manage to lower their volume by having a few drinks after work. I was relatively well, or so I believed. I was forty-two years old, had spent close to three decades in the mental health system, and figured that it was time to stand alone on my own two feet.

This sort of false confidence sabotages the recovery of many a person who suffers from mental illness, and I was no different. In fact, my sense of well-being was short-lived. Descending to the subway station at Eighth Avenue and Twenty-third Street on my way to work one morning, I was jostled by a group of teenaged boys who came charging down the stairs. Thrown off-balance, I thrust my left hand out to stop from going straight into a wall and suffered a compound fracture of my arm from elbow to wrist. At the hospital, doctors placed my arm in a cast, but the greater damage to me was psychological. I became convinced that the boys had been in cahoots with my voices, that they had purposely tried to harm me—to get the fat man—and that they'd try again. For a week after my accident, someone from the horticulture unit would have to accompany me to work and someone else would arrive at quitting time to ride home with me. I was *that* scared. But I continued to go to my job each day, and I believed I was doing well.

So I was totally unprepared when the copy room supervisor, a young black man, stopped by my station one day and said, "In a day or so, Fountain House will be bringing someone over for you to train."

"Oh?" I said, my heart racing.

"Your time will be up in two weeks," he said matter-of-factly.

Why was I being let go? What had I done wrong? I thought back to my job at Fairchild Publications, when I had first arrived in New York. After all these years, I was back in the city, practically around the corner from where I'd lived so long ago, and I was being fired again. I began to see old demons—Nick, Ted—stalking me.

Distraught, I went to talk to Bodil at Fountain House. Early on in my placement at NRDC, my employer had contacted Bodil and asked her to do something about my personal hygiene—I'd been rushing off to work without showering, and I smelled. She'd handled the matter gently. "Sweetheart, you have to make sure you're washed and clean before you leave your place," she'd said, and I didn't have to be told twice. I hoped she could make things right again.

As usual, Bodil was surrounded by people. I waited for a private moment and then told her without preamble, "They fired me."

She looked straight at me. "What do you mean, sweetie?" she asked. "What did you do?"

"I don't know," I said. "They're having someone come in to train for my job."

"Oh, no, sweetie, you're not being fired," Bodil said. She explained, "The job belongs to Fountain House, not to you. You've been there six months, now it's time for someone else to be trained. You'll come back here, hang around for a while, then we'll get you another job."

Bodil's explanation notwithstanding, my heart was broken. I had liked the work and welcomed the money. Within days, I became confused, disoriented, and easy prey for the voices, which told me again and again what a terrible failure I was. I began drinking heavily and at all hours in a vain effort to drown the evil spirits inside me, demons that kept saying I was too old to live, too gross to live, too stupid to live. Convinced by now that they were right, I began talking more and more about doing their bidding. I asked Alec, "What's the best way for a fat guy to end his life?" Alarmed, he told the Fountain House staff that I was hallucinating and talking about suicide again. They had me readmitted to Roosevelt Hospital, where I was given a medication that had me bouncing off the walls. After a week, I was discharged with a ten-day supply of whatever they had given me, and I returned to Alec's apartment.

I felt like Jell-O, couldn't keep a thought in my head for a minute, and would sit for long intervals, smoking, drooling, and dozing. I also quickly began drinking again to still the voices. One weekend, I disappeared. Alec went looking for me in one neighborhood beer joint after another. "What are you doing to yourself?" he demanded when he finally located me in a sleazy bar on Eighth Avenue. I couldn't answer. What I was doing, I knew as well as he, was destroying myself, dashing all that I had worked to achieve. "You don't want to go back to the hospital, do you?" he asked, looking straight into my bloodshot eyes. "Take a really hard look at these people around you," he said. I did. They were the usual sorry types—drifters, homeless types, guys on the make. "Is *this* how you see yourself?" Alec asked. "Is *this* what you want?"

I began to listen. Somebody cared, really cared about what happened to me. "No, I don't think so," I said haltingly.

"Then let's call Bodil and get you some help," Alec said, and we made the call.

"I'll go with you to the SSI office tomorrow and we'll reapply for benefits," Bodil said after I told her what was happening. "Now go home and get some rest. We'll try to get there when the office opens."

At eight the next morning, Bodil and I told my story to a clerk. We expected to have to begin the application procedure anew, a time-consuming operation, and were surprised and delighted when the clerk entered my Social Security number into the computer and found that my SSI application had been approved the previous month. I had one retroactive check waiting (because they had no address for me), and the others would be sent to me monthly. "You're eligible to receive Medicaid immediately," said the clerk. "All you need is proof of a correct mailing address."

"But what about my phone call canceling the application for SSI?" I blurted out.

"That's not the way to cancel an application," he told me. "How would anyone know that was really you on the phone?"

God had sent another of his angels. I supplied the necessary paper and received a temporary Medicaid card in the mail two days later.

Over the next year, I continued to room with Alec but felt a growing need for a place with my own name on the lease. I found a two-bedroom apartment in Park Slope, Brooklyn, obtained the necessary supported housing subsidy approval, and moved in with another member of the horticulture unit. Alec and I continued to meet socially and spend many memorable weeks and weekends working at High Point Farm. I'd never before tasted anything as sweet as corn that I ate the same day I picked it, never eaten tomatoes off the vine until I worked in the fields at Montague. It was hard work, but it came well rewarded.

I had another job as well. My new transitional employment placement, via Fountain House, was in the mail room at the *Village Voice,* a counterculture weekly with a diverse and devoted readership. I liked the people at the *Voice,* but the atmosphere was hectic. I soon found myself being given responsibilities outside the mail room—assisting the classifieds staff, running credit cards for approval, handling phones, and doing other office work. One night late in March, after working long hours helping to get the paper on press, I was standing on the subway platform, waiting for the F train that would take me home to Brooklyn. I was exhausted and tense. Suddenly, my voices began to accost me, shrieking in my ears as the subway roared into the station.

Working man . . . working slave, they wailed. *Think you're somebody special because they asked you to stay late? You're special because you come cheap. Face it, Kenny, you're a loser. . . . Jump off the platform, and the newspaper will still be published without you. Take one, two, three steps toward the edge. See the rails? It's the third rail you want, Kenny. The third rail will do the job. . . . Jump and they'll write about it in the paper. Jump now!*

Was it my exhaustion? The late hour? Had someone at the paper said something to touch off this assault from within? It could have been any of these things or all of them that threw me off-balance. I usually boarded the second or third car of the train because they were closest to the exit near my home. This time, dazed and disoriented, I stumbled along the platform and entered a car toward the rear. When I got off the train at my stop, nothing was familiar. I felt totally lost—as if I'd never seen the station before. No one looked safe.

A group of teenaged boys were headed in my direction, and I began breathing hard. They would hurt me. I knew it. They would push me against a wall. Like the last time, they'd break my arm. This time, they'd succeed in killing me. The voices agreed. *They're out to get you, Kenny,* they shouted in warning, and began to laugh their maniacal laughter. Panicked, I backed away through an exit and found myself trapped in a small, enclosed area. This part of the station was unmanned by a transit clerk at night; the entrance was closed. The young men had moved on without even a glance in my direction. I was alone behind a barred gate, much as I had been years before at Pueblo State Hospital. I began to sweat. My voices taunted me with experiences of years past. They carried me to every solitary room, every confinement I had ever been in. They had me back at the rape scene, and I heard myself begging, "Please, help me, somebody help me." But the walls did not answer.

Hours later, a transit guard making his rounds discovered me huddled in a corner. I'd stopped crying and sat hugging my chest for warmth and solace ... and to control the tremors that periodically coursed through my body. "You all right in there, fella?" the guard called to me. "Need help? Want me to call the police?"

"No," I said, trying to sound calm although my heart was racing. From past experience, I could imagine what would happen if the police were summoned. I'd find myself on the way to a hospital. But I knew something else this time. *I understood that I could stop that from happening!* It was amazing to realize that I wasn't just being driven by my voices but that I had some say over what happened to me. Though the voices were still with me—even as I spoke to the guard—I did not have to succumb to them . . . not this time. "I got into this jam by accident," I told the guard evenly, "and I'd be very grateful if you could get the key to open the door to the street so that I can get out." I strove to remain composed. "I can take it from there."

He did. And I did.

When I returned home, I mulled over the evening's events: the paralyzing paranoia and then . . . that one, wonderful moment when I managed to override the voices. I desperately wanted more such moments. At the very core of me, I knew that I had to get help—a good doctor, more effective medicine, I didn't know what—if I was to have any hope of getting better. (I never considered the possibility of getting *well,* but *better* suddenly seemed a not-altogether-impossible goal.) I don't remember what medication I was then taking, but it wasn't working. The voices continued to dominate every moment of my waking consciousness.

Desperate to find a more effective treatment, I signed in at the outpatient clinic at Roosevelt Hospital. This was not my first time there. At each visit, I'd see a different doctor. This time, the doctor was a man in his late thirties—too old to be an intern, I thought. He was clean shaven, had a full head of dark brown hair, and might have seemed pleasant enough, except that he looked bored. Without asking about my history (what medicines I'd been given, their different effects on me), he took out a pad and wrote out his prescription: Cogentin.

"I can't read when I'm on Cogentin," I told him after I'd looked at the prescription.

"The medicine is more important than reading," he responded flatly, turning away from me and beginning to clean the dirt from under his fingernails with the nails of his other hand. His nails were getting far more attention than his patient. I felt like shouting, "How dare you do this when I'm talking to you," but I took the prescription and left. I never had it filled. I returned two more times and tried to explain what I was going through to this same doctor—and he continued to brush me off. The voices were with me every day, and this doctor (a former gynecologist, I later learned) had no understanding of what was going on—how many voices there were, how insistent and insulting they could be. "Just stop listening to those voices," he told me on my third visit, as if he were lecturing an unruly schoolboy. "Discipline yourself."

Sick as I was, I was not going to tolerate this. I looked elsewhere for help, asking around for suggestions as to where I might go and whom I might see. Bonnie Bean, housing director at Fountain House and a woman who knows how to get things done, placed a call to a colleague who recommended a therapist and clinic near my home in Brooklyn. That phone call turned out to be the most important call of my life.

On a cool, crisp spring day in late April 1991, I rode the F train to the Seventh Avenue station in Brooklyn. On the way to the Park Slope Center for Mental Health, my voices warned me to be fearful of two men at the far end of the car. *Here's your chance to let someone else take your life for you,* said the voices. *Those two guys want to rob you, but if you put up a fight, they'll shoot or stab you to death.*

The train pulled into my station. I didn't move, waiting in suspense to see if the men would stay or go. I remained seated until the last second, then had to struggle to keep the doors open so I could exit. Neither man followed. My voices roared with laughter at my clumsy escape. *You should have died years ago in the forest when you had your first chance to kill yourself,* they chided me. *You are a grotesque freak,* they said, making their disgust clear. *Now your body is decomposing and beginning to reveal to everyone how ugly, hideous, and repulsive you've become since the day you were conceived.*

My body *was* grotesque. I had tripled in weight from the time I began taking prednisone for my asthma. I was breathless all the time and could barely exercise. I was ungainly. I no longer could bear to look at myself, to the point where I had begun to shave without using a mirror. I shied from seeing my reflection in shop windows. *Freak,* the voices shouted, and I agreed with them.

Out on the street now, I dug into my shirt pocket and took out a piece of paper that bore the name and address of the clinic: *Park Slope Center, 464 Ninth Street.* I walked up and down Ninth Street three times. It was a tree-lined street with rows of well-tended private residences. I didn't see any clinic. I was sure I'd been given the wrong address, and I checked once more. Number four sixty-four . . . The four-story brownstone bearing this address was indistinguishable from the other homes on the street except for a discreet brass plaque near the door that read: PARK SLOPE CENTER FOR MENTAL HEALTH, RITA SEIDEN, EXECUTIVE DIRECTOR.

I walked up a flight of steps to the entrance slowly. In all my years in the mental health system, I had never seen a center or clinic that looked anything like this building. The interior confirmed my impression. There were plants everywhere. Before me, a wood-banistered staircase led to a second floor. To the right on the first floor was the main reception area, with a carved ceiling, old brass chandelier, large fireplace, memento-filled mantelpiece, and chairs on which cushions had been strewn about; it looked like somebody's front parlor. I half expected to see gaslights.

A woman seated behind a desk toward the rear of the room greeted me. "Mr. Steele?" she inquired pleasantly.

I nodded and looked about me anxiously.

"Hello. I'm Ann," she continued. "You're a little early. Won't you be seated?"

I settled myself carefully on an antique bench and studied the framed photographs that filled the walls. My voices were talking among themselves, and I sat quietly, lulled by their sounds.

"Hello, Mr. Steele. My name is Rita Seiden."

I jumped. The speaker, a petite, pleasant-looking woman with warm brown eyes and wavy brown hair, looked down at me and smiled. She invited me into her office, which was separated from the reception area by a leaded glass door. The look and feel of the space continued and expanded on the sense of home that had marked the reception area. There was a Chinese screen, a soft leather couch, lots of artwork, and several diplomas—not just hers, but her father's and grandmother's as well. Most therapists keep their private life from their patients. This therapist shared her family. I felt that I entered her place as a guest, not a client.

Rita Seiden has a doctorate, but it is in sociology. In the early eighties, following a successful career as an academic, she decided that she wanted to be a therapist and attended the Adelphi School of Social Work, earning a master's degree in social work in 1983. She held a number of different jobs in the mental health field and opened the clinic, with psychiatrist Georges Casimir, in 1989.

During this first and subsequent meetings with Dr. Seiden, I talked endlessly, telling story after story. "Call me Shannon," I began, "but I'm officially known as K. Shannon Steele." . . . "My parents died in an airplane crash when I was young." . . . "I had an affair with a neighbor when I was fifteen and she was sixteen. We had a son, Joey. The mother died in childbirth. Her parents didn't want the baby," I ranted on, "so my parents raised Joey on their own." (It never fazed me that the same parents who died young in an airplane crash were now raising my son.) . . . "I held an important position in the office of Dianne Feinstein when she was mayor of San Francisco," I told Dr. Seiden, "and I challenge you to phone and check out my story." (To her credit, Dr. Seiden never made the call.) . . . "My father is a big executive in a steel firm, and my mother is very wealthy," I told the doctor. (Again we were talking about the same parents who had died so young and tragically in an earlier account.)

I paced the floor as I said these things, half believing them to be true. Joey *was* my son; my mother and father *had* died . . . at least they were dead to me. And I puffed one cigarette after another. When I smoked, Dr. Seiden asked me to step outside her office to a small balcony, where I continued to recount my preposterous stories.

She sat quietly, taking it all in. "That's part of what goes on with schizophrenia," she explained to me later in our relationship. "It's that the whole judgment is impaired, plus you have voices hectoring you, talking about your shortcomings, telling you that you are worthless. It's like having a constant headset on, at the same time that there are people making demands on you to have an ordinary life."

Rita Seiden was one of the few therapists I met who were truly interested in me, and I know I gave her a hard time. I made and canceled appointments. After a few months, I ran away from her probing questions. I liked to tell the stories *I* chose to talk about, but I didn't want to speak about my childhood, which is where she insisted we begin. Rita Seiden was like a good mother; she was clearly interested in me, and I felt myself about to succumb to her caring. The voices were threatened. I would talk to her, and the voices would be talking to me. *Leave at once!* The Ruler ordered.

I followed the voices.

I don't remember where they led me. I think I got a job helping out in a small grocery story and slept in the back for a while. I know that I spent much of the time homeless, living in upstate New York and Pennsylvania. During this period, I made several more stabs at ending my life. Confronting the majesty of Niagara Falls, I decided that I had found the perfect place to commit suicide—better than jumping off a building or throwing myself in front of a speeding truck. Way, way preferable to hanging from a tree. *Now, now I will do it,* I told myself as the spray of the falls bounced up to wet my face. But I didn't jump. Something indefinable drew me back to people who had helped me in the past and to places where I'd found comfort during the long odyssey of my illness. I returned to New York City.

In the summer of 1993, physically and mentally ill, I turned up at Fountain House. Housing coordinators Sandra Stocker and Luis Rivera placed me in temporary quarters in a ground-floor apartment nearby. Against my wishes, Luis took me to Roosevelt Hospital, where I was admitted for a few days. I remember being put on a medication that caused me to drool at the mouth and was so sedating that, after I left the hospital, I'd doze off while sitting on the rug in my friend Alec's living room as he and I were speaking. But I could not sleep at night. No sooner would I close my eyes than I'd be jolted awake by the terrifying images of my sorry life: my father's look of disappointment; The Ruler's voice; Nick and Ted's exploitation of me; the sounds and smells of the men who raped me; all the state ward bullies I'd had to confront. I would sit up, my mind racing, my body in a cold sweat, my voice screaming "NO!" I was afraid to close my eyes again . . . and so I lay in bed waiting for the dawn.

As soon as the effects of the medication wore off, I phoned Dr. Seiden. It was clear from the tone of the receptionist who answered the phone that my call wasn't welcome. I looked at Alec. "I don't think the doctor will take me back as a client," I said. "What will I do then?"

"Just try," he answered. "Things will work out."

The following day, Rita Seiden returned my call. I explained what I was experiencing, told her about my disenchantment with the people who had seen me at Roosevelt Hospital, and apologized for the disruption and tumult I had brought to her center. "I've been raised in state hospitals, and I don't know how to behave properly in a clinic like yours," I said, "but I'd like to try it one more time, if you'll have me."

"Come in tomorrow and we'll see how it goes," was all she would commit to.

Leaning on a cane and holding tight to the railing, I climbed the stone steps to the Park Slope Center for Mental Health. In the time I'd been away, my own health (which had not been good to start with) had grown much worse. I entered the foyer hesitantly. The place looked the same as before, except that the staff members weren't so quick to smile at my entrance.

Dr. Seiden greeted me with similar wariness.

"I want to come back and continue the hard work we were doing," I said. I also told her that coming back was something I never voluntarily did. The only reason I could give her, let alone myself, was that the "heart" of the place that I felt from my first visit had actually been strong enough to overcome the wishes and expressed commands of the schizophrenic voices that had been with me since the age of fourteen. "I'm not sure that I'll be able to resist them and stay this time," I said. "The best I can do is promise to try. Please, I'd like a second chance."

Dr. Seiden studied me in silence for a while. Her reply took some time to come. "Okay, we'll see how it goes," she finally said. "One session at a time."

I had my second chance and was determined not to botch it.

My medical problems required immediate attention, we both agreed, but I couldn't choose just any physician who came recommended nor look through the classified directory to find someone near my home. The challenge for me, as it is for so many others like me, was to identify good doctors who would accept Medicaid payments. Fortunately, the Health Insurance Plan (HIP) of New York was opening its membership to eligible Medicaid recipients, including, for a short time, people on SSI with Medicaid. I applied, was accepted, and soon found myself examined by a number of specialists, including Dr. Daniel Alpert (who remains my internist to this day), pulmonary specialist Dr. Jane E. Levitt, plus a cardiologist and a diabetes specialist. Each discovered medical problems that needed to be treated. Dr. Levitt, in particular, will always have my gratitude. It was she who ordered sleep apnea testing for me at St. Luke's Hospital on October 27, 1994. The results showed that my nightly sitting up, falling over, and head-banging (which the doctors at Manhattan Psychiatric Center had dismissed as another failed suicide attempt) *weren't* all in my head. I do indeed suffer from sleep apnea and require the help of a special machine that delivers air through a mask placed over my nose at a pressure greater than that of the surrounding air. This continuous positive airway pressure (CPAP) opens the upper airway passages. Dr. Levitt's persevering efforts to get me the machine I needed, and continue to use, have saved my life.

I credit other doctors, and a different medication, with helping to restore my sanity.

Back in therapy with Rita Seiden, I told her that I was no longer taking any antipsychotic medication. "I've been through them all," I explained. "I'd rather live with my voices than suffer the horrific side effects from the meds."

"I can understand your disappointment," she said. "Still, I'd like you to see our medical director, Georges Casimir."

My first appointment with the doctor took place in August 1994. A slim, handsome man whose speech retained the lilt of his native Haiti, Dr. Casimir examined me, took down my history, and heard my concerns about the various medicines I had been given in the three decades since I'd first been visited by the voices. Like Rita Seiden, he wasn't dismissive. He paid careful attention to what I had to say.

"There's something I would like you to try," Dr. Casimir said when I'd finished speaking. "It's called Risperdal (chemical name: risperidone). I know you distrust medicines, but this is one of a new generation of drugs called atypical antipsychotic medications. They're reputed to have fewer side effects than the medicines that were prescribed in the past. Early reports are encouraging.

"If you don't like it, you can stop taking it," he added. No other doctor had ever given me that choice.

I agreed to try the medicine, but I took a lower dosage than was prescribed. One of the reasons I did what Dr. Casimir suggested, albeit in my fashion, was that he was very clear about what he was going to do and asked for my cooperation. Doctors don't get compliance by ordering people around: Do this; take this. They need to have a partnership with the patient. I wasn't forced to take the medicine, and because I wasn't forced, I agreed to take it.

Dr. Casimir was right; there were fewer side effects. I felt somewhat sedated, but that grew less pronounced as my system became used to the medication. And I did, and still do, have to deal with dryness of mouth and constipation. But I was able to function.

During this time, I acquired a place of my very own, a one-bedroom apartment just a few blocks from my friend Alec's home. The thought of living without a roommate was frightening. What if I got sick? What if the voices continued to torment me? What if they told me to commit suicide and I gave in to them? In therapy, Dr. Seiden and I worked through these fears.

And so I made the move, taking along my black cat, Diva, who came into my life when I was temporarily placed in the ground-floor apartment, and adding first one aquarium and then another—later to be joined by a canary, which lives in a cage next to my bedroom window. I filled my place with life. I was fortunate in having the services of a housekeeper, Maria Rivera, provided by Medicaid to help maintain me in the "least restrictive, most cost-effective environment in the community." My physical ailments make shopping, cleaning, and cooking difficult. Maria comes by three times a week to help me out with these tasks and to bring good cheer. In November 1994, I started to take my medication every single day.

That same month, I approached Dr. Seiden with a request. In order to remain a member in good standing at Fountain House, I had to be involved in a structured activity, such as the day treatment programs to which I'd been assigned. I wanted to replace these sequential jobs with an individual project, which would be sanctioned and supervised by Dr. Seiden. My idea was to create and run a voter registration project for the last disenfranchised constituency in America: the mentally ill. As a volunteer on the Feinstein campaign so many years earlier, I'd seen how important it was to bring out the vote. I'd worked on phone banks, had called registered voters to make sure they knew the location of their polling site, and had even gone out to help voters who had difficulty in getting to the polls. I would do that now for a cause, not a candidate.

I had prepared my argument. "No one just gave women the vote in 1920," I told Dr. Seiden. "They had to fight for it. Similarly, one of the early goals of the civil rights movement of the 1960s was the elimination of barriers to the voting booth. It had been a struggle. These voting rights, and others, were not secured until the Voting Rights Act of 1965, which suspended state voter qualification tests. In 1971, the Twenty-sixth

Amendment lowered the voting age to eighteen. If you were old enough to fight for our country, the reasoning went, you were old enough to vote for its leaders. Further, no one needs to pay to vote in America today or to pass any test of literacy. If you can sign your name with an *X*, you can vote.

"Being mentally ill and being mentally incompetent are not the same thing," I declared. "Why, then, should we who are mentally ill remain politically silent when there's so much at stake that could affect the quality of our lives?"

What got me so excited about the project was that I'd recently begun hearing new voices—in addition to the voices of The Ruler and his legions. These new voices spoke to me from the radio and television, as voices had done from the time I was fourteen, but now there was an important difference. The new voices were *real*. And riveting. They were also extraordinarily frightening.

They spoke of abandoning disadvantaged people, including the mentally ill—including me. They wanted to take away all our support systems, to eliminate our meager SSI, SSD (Social Security Disability), and Medicaid payments. They demanded cutbacks in community mental health services, treatment, housing, and research. They expected us, the mentally ill, somehow to pull ourselves up by our own bootstraps. If we failed, we could wind up homeless or in jail. It mattered little to these political voices. They simply did not want our care to cost them money.

I also heard the voice of Mario Cuomo, then governor of New York, when he spoke at Fountain House in December 1993 on the occasion of his signing the Mental Hygiene Reinvestment Act, which says that money made from the sale of state hospital properties should be reinvested in community mental health services. Governor Cuomo said that his decision to sign the act was "a good and compassionate thing to do, but not a smart political act since the mentally ill don't vote and those opposed to my signing this act do." When Cuomo lost the election, I was angry. I believed that he lost because he had defended a group that couldn't reward his courage.

The mentally ill don't vote. I vowed to change that situation. In November 1994, I began the Mental Health Voter Empowerment Project, with Dr. Seiden's blessing. In New York City, postage-paid voter registration cards are available from the Board of Elections. Upstate, voter registration forms do require stamps. I obtained a supply of the appropriate cards and forms, then found my way to the shelters and other housing where many mentally ill people live and to the clubhouses and day treatment programs where they congregate. In addition to the forms, I took with me a folding table, a tablecloth printed in red, white, and blue, and some small American flags. My efforts were educational and completely nonpartisan. I was a traveling salesman, and what I was selling was a key to the ballot box.

In the years since, I've been praised for the innovative nature of this project, but what I really liked about it was that it was comfortingly monotonous. All I had to do, once I reached a residence or meeting place, was set up my table and sit there—just sit there, talk to people, and help them to register as voters. The reason such rote work was welcome is that my delusional voices were still with me then. It's hard to have a conversation when there are conversations going on in your head. I had a set argument about why voting is important, and I could make that argument again and again. When people actually registered and made a choice about voting, that was the real empowering act because they then could make other choices: Should I take my medication or not? Should I work or not? Should I take responsibility or not?

My original goal was to engage about 300 people. By November 1996, with the help of seventy-five volunteers whom I recruited in Manhattan and Brooklyn, close to 8,500 new voters had been registered throughout the five boroughs. During the fall, volunteers had reached more than 7,700 of these voters, making sure they knew the location of their polling sites and even helping many get to the polls. To date, more than 35,000 people with serious mental illness have registered to vote in New York City alone, most of them for the first time in their lives. The project has gone national and is currently under way in thirty-six states. The challenge remains, and the work goes on.

During the months I was building the project, Dr. Seiden noted that our therapy sessions were going better. I was pacing less and reflecting more. She jotted this down in her notes. In fact, my delusional voices had been receding, but I'd been too busy to notice. Thus I was totally unprepared for what happened next.

On May 3, 1995, sitting on my living room sofa, with Diva resting cozily in my lap, I made a startling discovery.

My voices had stopped.

{ 8 }

The Day the Voices Stopped

ONE MINUTE THE VOICES were babbling away; the next they were gone—replaced by a persistent, mantra-like *om* from the living room air conditioner. *Something must be wrong with it,* I thought. Gently lifting Diva from my lap, I stood, walked quickly across the room, and turned the air conditioner off . . . only to then be accosted by a loud *whir* from the electric motor connected to my newly installed tropical fish aquarium and the *drip-drip-drip* of water, like the steady beat of a drum, trickling from the filter into the tank. The hum of the light in the hood of the aquarium was joined by a buzzing noise from the overhead fluorescent light.

I turned off the lights and ran into the bedroom, my cat following closely. From outside the bedroom windows, which face a heavily trafficked avenue, a cacophony of city noises invaded my space: screeching brakes, wailing sirens, car horns blaring at full volume. I covered my head to stifle the earsplitting sounds. Then, removing my hands from my ears, I became keenly aware of the constant ticking of the three clocks I'd brought with me to the apartment.

The telephone rang. Once, twice . . . The rings sounded like fire alarms. I had heard this same phone ring a few hours before, and it hadn't been this loud, just as I'd been aware of the street noises earlier and had not been distracted by them. I didn't answer the phone but yanked the cord from the wall.

I was being *bombarded* by the everyday noises—discordant notes that had remained in the background all the while my hallucinatory voices took center stage. Now I was encircled by them, engulfed by quadraphonic sound. My chest tightened. My body grew wet with perspiration.

I turned on the television and radio, switching from channel to channel and station to station in a frantic attempt to tune my voices back in. I *wanted* them to return! For thirty-two years, they had been my constant companions. Even when I was homeless, they lived with me. Although they had criticized and insulted me, ordered me to abandon new relationships and quit safe harbors, and constantly commanded me to kill myself, these same haunting voices had also made it seem as if the sun rose and set on me. Epimenides, a Cretan seer who lived in the sixth century B.C., is reputed to have said, "There is a pleasure in being mad which none but the madmen know." I *knew*. The voices had conferred a specialness to my existence. Without them, I felt very much alone.

Desperate, I switched the TV dial to a channel filled with snow and white sound, and I turned the volume up, hoping to mask all the other noises. Slumped on my living room floor in front of the screen, I tried to make sense of the voices' disappearance. What if they had given up on telling me to kill myself and abandoned me to my fate? What if I was heading straight for hell and no longer needed them to show me the way? What lay before me? How would I deal with it? What if they were truly gone and, with them, the world as I'd known it for more than thirty years? What would I do? How would I function?

Later that evening, I walked into the bathroom and locked the door. Fully dressed, I wedged my body into the tub, drew the sliding glass doors shut, and lay down in a fetal position. I felt like a deer that knows the hunter has him in his sights and is powerless to move. Numb with fear, I remained locked in that bathroom for three sleepless days and nights. The constant cries of my cat, whom I hadn't fed in all this time, finally brought me from the room. I opened a can of food and spooned it into her bowl. Then I crawled into bed and slept for forty-eight hours straight, Diva curled at my feet. When Maria came to clean the place, she couldn't wake me.

The voices were back.... They were babbling in a foreign language. I didn't know what they were saying.... I was being strangled by them....

Gasping for air, I woke to find that, in my restlessness, I'd disconnected the tubing between my face mask and the CPAP machine, making breathing a struggle. I'd had a nightmare. My voices had not returned. And I was in my own bed in my own apartment. I forced myself to get up, to wash, to eat, to keep an appointment with my therapist.

I did not immediately tell Dr. Seiden that the voices had stopped, although I'd begun to tell her many other things about my life, starting with the revelation that my name was Ken, not Shannon. Little by little, and over a long period, I gave her as much truth as I was able to recall, along with many of my fears. She helped me confront my feelings about my family: my mother's coldness, the knowledge that I had disappointed my father, the birth of a "replacement" when I was fifteen. Each case of schizophrenia is a different mix of genetic and psychological factors, and I was striving to come to terms with my story. The work was hard and painful.

At one of my appointments following the departure of my voices, Dr. Seiden remarked on some changes that she'd noted in my behavior. "You've always been articulate," she said, "but you seem uncharacteristically lucid and clear today. Your eye contact is better, and your attention is more focused. You seem to have listened to my questions more carefully and responded to them in less convoluted ways." She sat back in her chair, looked thoughtfully at me, and asked, "How's the new medication doing?"

How's the new medication doing? I repeated her question to myself.

"Ken, are you here?" Dr. Seiden asked. "You seem to have faded away."

"Sorry," I said. "I didn't sleep well last night." I still said nothing about the voices' absence.

Dr. Seiden wasn't the only one who had my attention. For the first time in decades, I was free to hear the voices of others, even when they weren't speaking to or about me. No longer well enough to take buses and trains—I was grossly overweight, had a serious heart condition, severe asthma, diabetes, and had suffered two serious falls that required hospitalization—I traveled by ambulette (a van for disabled persons) to and from doctors' appointments. When my voices had been active, I'd sat silently, absorbed in listening to their auditory commands and paying heed to no one else unless they directed my attention elsewhere. They controlled everything I thought, about myself and other people. Now I heard my fellow passengers speak in varied accents of their worries and concerns, discuss the weather or sports, tell jokes. At times, I even found myself laughing at their stories. No one glared back at me in anger or said demeaning things to me. Not one of the passengers was out to get me. Without my schizophrenic voices, I had become just another man—but, thank God, no longer a marked man.

Good morning, Mr. Steele." I was greeted by a small, white-haired woman as I stood in the lobby, opening my mailbox.

"Hi," I replied.

"You're new here, aren't you?" said my elderly neighbor, who then began a monologue on the history of the building, the foibles of the other tenants, her problems with management. Standing there, I realized with some amazement that this was the first time since the onset of my illness that I'd heard gossip about anyone other than myself. *Aren't I worth attention anymore?* I thought. But I listened courteously, even saying a sentence or two when the woman paused. I was learning how to make small talk.

The struggle to make it on my own was a different matter. Like my doctor and those with whom I worked on the Mental Health Voter Empowerment Project, many people were now beginning to see me as an articulate grown man, but in fact I felt like a child—an adult child. Ordinary tasks were as challenging to me as solving the mystery of the universe to others. Although I'd worked in many kitchens over the years, those places had been fully stocked, and all I'd had to do was cook. Organizing my own kitchen was another matter. Now it was up to me to figure out: Where do the glasses go? Where do I put the groceries? Then, *after* I had everything in place, someone told me about paper shelving, so I had to clear the shelves, put paper down, then put everything back. I'd drop cups of coffee and, picking up the broken pieces, I'd feel as if I were holding my broken life in my hands.

I kept silent about the absence of my voices in part because I thought their disappearance might be temporary. But I also kept the knowledge to myself because I wanted to preserve my options: to return to a world that I knew, one in which I was cared for, or to remain voice free and face the challenges of a new life. The freedom that came with being "normal" was threatening. Like many others, I had become system-addicted, and I knew just how to work the system. Protected by the mental health establishment, on which I depended to structure and organize all aspects of my life, I had learned which passwords to utter and which behaviors to display in order to be hospitalized; I understood what I needed to do in order to gain ground privileges; I knew my way around halfway houses. I knew outpatient clinics, community residences, and the cloistered and safe clubhouse communities like Fountain House, which expected the least of me and not the most. During the first few months of being well, many people who have suffered from hallucinations quickly get unwell. System-addiction is often the cause. It needs to be recognized so that it can be addressed and combated.

Dr. Seiden's question came back to me. *How's the new medication doing?* She had been concerned primarily about side effects, but I began to wonder about substance. *Could the new medicine be what was responsible for controlling my voices?* Over the years, I had heard that promise made about one pill after another, and none of them had worked. I felt a need to know more about what I was taking.

Janssen Pharmaceutica, which manufactures Risperdal, has a toll-free information line. In September 1995, I placed a call to it.

"May I help you?" said the woman who answered.

"I have a close friend who has been diagnosed as a paranoid schizophrenic," I said. "He became ill in his early teens and has heard voices for over thirty years. He is taking Risperdal. Recently, his voices stopped completely. Can this drug actually stop hallucinatory voices?"

"Yes, it can," said the woman. "It has successfully stopped auditory and visual hallucinations for many patients."

So now I knew. And it was time to share the news. I wrote a letter to Dr. Casimir. In it, I said: *Thank you for convincing me to try this medication. You didn't lie to me. The side effects are minimal. You've given me back my life. I don't know what I'm going to do with it, but you've given me a second chance.*

On September 25, during a regular therapy session, I told Dr. Seiden that the voices were gone. I tried not to make a big deal over it, but when she took the news calmly, I was disappointed.

"When did this happen?" she asked.

"May third, 1995," I replied. "At first, I panicked and locked myself in the bathroom. Now I'm very suspicious about why they left and where they've gone."

"Where do you think they've gone?" she asked, leaning back in her chair.

"I think they may be playing some kind of game with me," I answered. I didn't know whether to say anything more but found myself blurting out, "I think the new medicine, Risperdal, may have stopped the voices."

"Well, we'll have to talk more about it in your next session," said Dr. Seiden. "Time has run out."

Her lack of reaction to my dramatic announcement threw me into confusion. Now I wasn't sure that it *was* the medication—or that the voices had gone away. I began to expand on an earlier thought: that the voices were visiting others and plotting traps for me. They were out there, commanding others to kill me. (In that case, I was still the center of the universe!) I grew paranoid in the extreme, locking and double-locking my front door, making sure the windows to my apartment were closed, and jumping every time the doorbell rang.

Dr. Seiden's notes on this period, which she shared with me years later, provide an interesting commentary on what was happening to me at this stage of my illness and how she perceived it. I cite them here with her permission:

Ken told me today that his voices had stopped. Absence of voices in a patient who has them is not in my scope of experience. It is true that Ken seemed less preoccupied with voice activity during our sessions. Prior to a few months ago, he would stop in the middle of a sentence, and close his eyes. At first I had asked him what was going on when he closed his eyes. He would reply that it was voice activity. By September, I had noticed the interruptions in our sessions were not occurring. Nevertheless, I had not concluded that the voice activity was gone. As with other symptoms or problems, sometimes they don't show in the session, but they do show in more stressful situations.

Not insignificantly, my accumulated experience and mentoring has supported the idea that antipsychotics quiet the psychotic symptoms but certainly don't end them. Take the case of Mrs. Smith. She was floridly psychotic with delusions of grandeur when I met her. Dr. Casimir medicated her with one of the traditional medications. One day I remarked to Dr. Casimir that the delusions seemed not to be there. He smiled at me and said, "You will find them just below the surface. You will have to ask about them." Sure enough, when I asked Mrs. Smith she said that she didn't talk about those ideas anymore because she knew people did not believe her.

Given the mix of fact, fiction, and delusion Ken had provided, I suspected that his more florid "stuff" was still "there" but under better control. This greater control would represent an improvement, but would be less of a miracle than the disappearance of the voices. . . . I wanted to talk to Dr. Casimir about whether Ken's improvement was possible. My consultation with him educated me to an emerging class of anti-psychotics that could indeed control symptoms like auditory hallucinations. Then I was prepared to believe in the absence of the voices.

Having shared my "miracle" with the doctors, I now felt compelled to pass the news along to just about everyone in my life—telling would make it even more real. In addition, publicity served as an insurance policy of sorts. It gave me added motivation to stay with the medicine.

At about this time, Fountain House asked me to participate in a panel at the American Psychiatric Association's annual Community Psychiatric Institute, to be held in Boston in the early part of October. I belonged to a Friday-morning group at Fountain House that dealt with housing problems in the clubhouse community and attempted to find solutions, which was the subject of the workshop. The group's leader picked me up the morning of October 7, and together we drove along Connecticut Route 84E toward Boston. As we passed a sign announcing an upcoming exit, ROUTE 69/PROSPECT, the pleasure I'd been taking in the drive and in seeing the colors of fall quickly turned to pain, confusion, nausea—a sweep of emotions and feelings. If we exited here, I could be at my parents' doorstep in less than fifteen minutes. Feigning car sickness, I asked the driver to stop briefly at the side of the road. I didn't tell him that I knew this area all too well.

Later, arriving at our destination, the three-star Boston Marriott Copley Place, I could not help but reflect on the last time I had been in this city. Then, the South End and its soup kitchens had been the part of town where I hung out before moving on to Massachusetts' state hospitals. It seemed like yesterday in some ways—but also like a thousand lifetimes ago. I resolved that I would use my new life to help improve conditions for other people with mental illness.

The panel, on October 9—my forty-seventh birthday—went well. The group leader and I were joined by two psychiatrists from New York's Roosevelt Hospital; we explained how our model, in which psychiatrists work along with clubhouse staff and mental health consumers to solve day treatment and residential problems, could be replicated. In telling my story, I shared the fact that Risperdal had successfully stopped my voices, adding that (like many others in my situation) I was now faced with allaying new fears and meeting new challenges in the constant struggle to stay well. I was like the Ancient Mariner, with a tale I had to tell.

When the presentation was over, a public relations professional approached me on behalf of the National Alliance for the Mentally Ill (NAMI) and asked if I would appear in a public service announcement. NAMI is the nation's leading self-help and family advocacy organization dedicated to improving the lives of people with severe mental illness; if I appeared in the alliance's announcement, titled "Fighting the War Against Mental Illness," my story would be known across America. Did I want to be that publicly identified as a schizophrenic? I thought quickly about the stigma connected with this illness and the need for those of us who suffer from it to identify ourselves and speak out. In a way, this was an extension of the Voter Empowerment Project. We need to be heard *and* seen. I swallowed hard and said I would do it. The crew came to my apartment to shoot my segment later that week.

Perhaps it was my growing public visibility, perhaps it was the fact that it was autumn (my favorite time of year), perhaps it was the drive to Boston and passing the exit to my hometown. For any of these reasons, and perhaps for all of them, I began to think about reconnecting with my family. The idea would not leave me. Were they still living in Prospect? Was their phone number still unlisted, as it had been when I'd called from Pueblo State Hospital?

I dialed information, gave the name and address, and was told their number—just like that. The ease of getting this information was so unexpected, it took my breath away. I jotted the phone number down in my address book, which I still use. It is written in a shaky hand. Ten digits now separated me from contact with my parents, whom I hadn't seen in twenty years. I agonized for nights, weighing whether to make the call.

My last encounter with the family had been a disaster, to say the least. How would my father and mother take hearing from me again? Should I leave them alone and not intrude in their lives after so many years and so much pain? Or should I let them know where I was and that I was doing well? I told myself that I wouldn't be calling because I needed something from them, but that was far from the truth.

Finally, in the middle of a sleepless night, I realized I was becoming obsessive about making the call. I had to stop this compulsive debating and do something about it. The following morning, at an hour when I knew my parents would be awake, I dialed the number.

God, please let them be receptive to my call, I prayed as I listened to the phone ring, once, twice . . .

"Hello." I heard my father's voice.

I closed my eyes as I replied, "Hi, Dad. It's your son, Ken."

There was a long silence. Finally, my dad asked, "How are you?"

"Better, Dad. Much better," I said, surprised to hear the evenness of my voice. I explained the reason for my feeling better, that I was taking a new medicine that had stopped my voices and brought my illness under control. I reassured him that I wasn't calling because I needed anything. I asked if I could see him, my mother, and Joey.

"I'll tell your mother you called and see how she feels about it," my father said. "Your brother is another matter. He's married, has two children, and he'll have to decide for himself if he wants to see you again."

Joey, a father? In my mind's eye, my brother was still an adolescent trying to decide between playing baseball or football. Now he was probably tossing a ball to his own kids.

"When will you let me know?" I asked, keeping my voice steady. My whole body was trembling now. If my heart went any faster, it would drive itself out of my chest, down, and onto the street two floors below my bedroom windows.

"This time next week," he replied, and hung up.

I collapsed on my bed, buried my face in my pillow, and sobbed.

It took some time for me to recover. When I did, the things that had been said (and left unsaid) in our brief conversation kept running through my mind. I was disappointed by my father's response. *But do I deserve any better?* I asked myself. Although we hadn't discussed the events of 1975, they were there between us, brought back to life and newly painful. This was one of my first real-world lessons in communicating: understanding that the unsaid often says more than what's spoken.

In the week that followed, I steeled myself for rejection. *Your parents won't want to see you,* I told myself, time and again, in the third person. *You don't deserve it. At least they know you're okay.* I said this so often, I almost believed I could live with a negative response.

When I called home the next week, my dad still had no answer for me, but he took my phone number. "I told Joey about your call," he said. "That's the best I can do." We spoke more easily now, and I thought, *Well, if all we do is keep in touch via the phone, that will be enough.* I also learned another big lesson in life: In the real world, there are two different kinds of feelings: those in your gut, which you have to honestly confront and resolve, and those in your head, which you rationalize and justify without satisfaction. What I wanted from the relationship with my parents (indeed, what I still want) was much more than what I could talk myself into accepting.

Three days later, my father called. "Your mother and I would like to see you and celebrate your birthday belatedly," he said. "We'll come into Manhattan." (For my dad, that was as dramatic an announcement as saying, "We'll fly over to Paris." He wasn't comfortable in the city. Who knows? Perhaps he would have been more uneasy about my showing up at his place in Connecticut.) We made a date to get together the first week in November.

I should have been delighted by the news, but I was in turmoil. Past history became caught up in present expectations as I tried to deal with a multitude of emotions: anger, guilt, failure, sadness, excitement, expectation, rejection, acceptance, betrayal, and hope all at the same time. I became so frightened and confused, I almost called my father back to cancel our reunion. I was terrified that I might suffer a serious setback in my illness and desperately wanted to turn to my therapist for help in managing this crisis, but my deception had closed that door. As far as Dr. Seiden knew, my parents were dead.

In an attempt to lessen the pressures building up in me, I wrote my thoughts down in the form of a letter to myself. It began:

> Dear Ken:
> It's all right for you to feel angry and betrayed by your parents—and still want to see them. It's all right for you to feel guilt, sadness, and failure because of all the disappointments you've brought to your parents—and still want to see them; it's all right, go ahead and be

excited about their coming, even if you fear that your father will say something that angers you. You won't rise to the bait. It's all right, Ken. You now have the self-control to listen to your father's anger, if he decides to express it, and love him and be pleased that he brought himself and your mother to see you. . . .

It took twenty more pages to convince myself that I had the impulse control to manage whatever would come.

The day of my parents' visit was clear and cool—the kind of day I have always loved. Fortunately, it was also a day when my housekeeper, Maria, was in. Together, she and I got the apartment tidy and sparkling. The woodsy smell of Old English Furniture Polish filled the air as I walked down the stairs from my apartment to the street, two and a half hours before my parents were due to arrive, and waited for them. I spent the entire time pacing back and forth from my house to the corner—a distance of some eight yards.

Finally, a car pulled up. My father leaned out the driver's window, spotted me, and asked where to park—"Someplace reasonable," he said. There's no such thing as an inexpensive parking garage in my neighborhood—New York's theater district—but I opened the back door, got into the car, and directed him to the best-priced lot in the area. Once we got out of the car, I shook my father's hand and lightly kissed my mother's cheek. My parents, older now, were clearly tired from the drive. Slowly, we made our way back to my house.

We walked up the flight of stairs to my apartment. My friend Alec had made a special wreath of eucalyptus leaves for the occasion, hoping it would bring me luck. I had hung it outside the door (where it is to this day). Hearing our voices, Maria opened the door wide to welcome us in. The tour of my place didn't take long. "Very nice," said my father as he settled down before the TV set. "Do you mind if I check the sports news?" I didn't mind, and he turned the set on, quickly locating the sports channel. Perhaps he, too, had been anxious about today's meeting and was soothed by the voices of familiar sports commentators, turning to them to fill the awkward silence that lay between the two of us.

Mom made herself a cup of coffee and sat drinking it at the dining table. She opened her purse. "I brought you pictures of Joey's family," my mother said, handing me two five-by-seven photos: one of my brother and his wife; the second of their two daughters.

My father looked away from the TV for a moment. "Beautiful kids, yes?" he said.

"You bet, Dad," I said. But I wasn't looking at the little girls. I was holding the picture of my brother. I was thinking how much he had aged.

We passed the photographs to Maria, who smiled approvingly. "Very pretty," she said.

"Do you have any children?" my mother asked her.

"Yes, and many grandchildren," Maria replied. She and Mom laughed together. I was glad that Maria was there on the day my parents had come to visit me. It lightened the mood. Finally, my father turned off the television and announced that they had better go. He handed me an envelope. Inside was a beautiful card and some money. I told him I was fine and didn't need the money. "It's for your birthday," he replied. I thanked him and offered to walk him and my mother back to the parking lot. "It's not necessary," he said.

At the door, he turned and said, "We'll come back at Christmastime. Call us and we'll set a date."

Then they were gone. The entire visit had lasted under an hour, but I thought about it for a long time thereafter. Nothing serious had been said. On the other hand, nothing terrible had taken place. All in all, I decided, it was a reasonably good first step toward our new relationship.

Another important relationship was on my mind—the one between me and my therapist. It was time to further unravel some of the many stories I'd been telling Dr. Seiden during the course of our work together. Once she realized how much of my fictionalized life I'd presented as fact, would she still want to work with me? I had to take that chance. I didn't want to live with those stories any longer. Fortunately, I didn't have much time to spend worrying over the "what-ifs" of the situation. Our next session was scheduled for the morning following my parents' visit.

I sat forward on the couch. "I have some important things to tell you today," I began, struggling to gaze directly at Dr. Seiden, when I would have been far more comfortable hiding behind the screen in her office.

She smiled warmly. "Are they good things?"

I hesitated as if they might not have been, but of course they were. "My parents came to visit me at my new apartment yesterday," I said, the words coming in a rush.

"So these were ghosts who visited?"

"No, my parents are alive," I said. I looked down at the rug. "Dr. Seiden, I have so many things to straighten out with you now, I don't know where to start."

She laughed, then responded to my unasked question. "No, Ken, I'm not laughing *at* you. I'm very pleased that you're able to tell me the truth. It's a breakthrough. You should be pleased as well."

I went on to say that Joey wasn't dead, either, and that he was my brother (not the son born to me from a tragic, teenaged affair), who was married and had two children. "My father says he can't speak for my brother's decision about seeing me or not," I told my doctor. "What do you think that means?"

"I don't know," she replied. "I don't know your brother."

Alas, I don't know him, either. Because of our age gap and because of my illness, I was quickly out of my brother's life. Then there was my terrible visit home, when Joey wasn't yet a teenager. Others with mental illness do not have that same history with their siblings, yet they still find themselves estranged from brothers and sisters who are "normal." Healthy siblings often suffer when the family's attention is focused on the person with the illness, and many grow up resenting that person. In addition, everyone worries that lightning will strike twice, that someone else in the family will develop a mental illness. I've come to believe that my brother worries less about himself than about his children—about whether they will be stricken with this illness. And so he keeps himself and them away from me. I feel very sad about this. Schizophrenia is not catching.

Dr. Seiden did not know about my last visit home, for I hadn't shared that dark period with her. A lot more of my story needed to be to told, changed, or clarified before my therapist could help me negotiate the maze of my life so that I could become the Ken Steele I wanted to be. We are still working on it.

The next relationship to be reconciled was with my God. Thanksgiving and Christmas were coming, and I had much to be thankful for. I'd discovered St. Malachy's Church, a warm and friendly parish near my home, but while still in the guise of an orphan I felt that I could not enter a holy place. (I didn't need the voices to tell me I was lying.) *I have sinned, Father. . . .* Now I could say those words and ask for absolution. I lit candles, asking that God's blessing be bestowed upon my parents, my brother and his family, and my friends, and I lit a candle in remembrance of my beloved grandmother. I thanked God for rescuing me from the devil. I felt blessed.

The day after Thanksgiving, a friend drove me to New Jersey, where I bought an eight-foot blue spruce and brought it back to my home. Friends lent me trimmings for the tree, and my mother and father—who returned, as promised, to celebrate with me—brought with them ornaments that had been hung on the trees of my childhood. My parents' second visit was more comfortable for us all, and we now look forward to being together on my birthday and at Christmas each year.

In addition, I set aside a day during the holiday season for friends to share God's bounty with me. The Christmas party has become an annual tradition, and each year I wonder how much more my walls can stretch to accommodate the growing number of guests—mental health consumers and professionals, neighbors and friends—who squeeze into my small place in a spirit of abundance and goodness.

But no Christmas was more special than the one that came after the voices went away, the Christmas when I was reunited with my Lord and gave thanks to all the people in my life who made up my new family—including my parents. I knew that I would not return to the voices. I also knew what I was going to do with this second chance that had been given me.

I vowed that I would use my own voice, in whatever ways I could, to make life better for myself and others who struggle, each day, to survive schizophrenia and other devastating diseases of the mind. I would listen to, and learn from, the voices of other mentally ill people and their families. Working together, we *could* make a difference. And we would be heard.

{ 9 }

Other People's Stories

THE PARK SLOPE CENTER for Mental Health published a newsletter for staff and clients of the agency. I asked Dr. Seiden if I could be its editor. My intent, I told her, was to widen the publication's coverage, expand its readership, and publicize the Mental Health Voter Empowerment Project. She gave permission, and so *Park Slope Center News* was redesigned and renamed *New York City Voices: A Consumer Journal for Mental Health*. My hope was that *voices* could now become a positive noun—one that clarifies distortion instead of the other way around. I felt hopeful in starting this new venture.

In November 1995, we published a four-page inaugural issue (circulation: 2,500) that focused on that month's political elections. Then, as now, our editorial policy had been to inform readers, not direct them. This is accomplished by presenting different points of view on a given issue, much as the goal of the Voter Empowerment Project is to bring voters to the polls, not tell them which levers to pull down once they're in the voting booth. The tabloid-sized newspaper, which is still operated as a program of the Park Slope Center for Mental Health, currently runs thirty-two pages and has a circulation of 40,000.

From the beginning, *New York City Voices* has reported to its readers on legislative issues that directly affect the quality of their lives. One matter that we continue to cover, for example, is mental health parity. According to a 1999 report issued by the U.S. surgeon general, one in every five Americans experiences a mental disorder in any given year, and half of all Americans have such disorders at some time in their lives, yet most never seek treatment. Some hold back because of the stigma of mental illness. (Nobody wants to be thought of, or to go on record, as being "crazy.") But many others fail to get the help they need because they lack the insurance to cover it.

This is where parity comes in. For years, the prevailing attitude of insurance companies toward mental health coverage was: If we can't see it, we don't have to pay for it. But the families involved have no trouble seeing the illness—they live with it day in and day out, as they witness their children slipping further and further from reality. And many of them *are* paying for it, by mortgaging their homes, businesses, and the futures of their other children in order to obtain the care and services that the affected young people need but that insurance will not cover. True, illnesses such as schizophrenia, bipolar disease, and major clinical depression don't show up, like cancer, on a biopsy or, like heart disease, on an EKG, but they are just as real. The fight for parity seeks to bridge the enormous gap between how physical ailments and mental illnesses are covered.

At the time of this writing, thirty-two states have passed some form of parity legislation, mostly limiting coverage to very serious illnesses such as schizophrenia, bulimia, and clinical depression. We need recognition and reimbursement for a wider range of conditions, and we need that to happen in all fifty states.

Most striking about *New York City Voices,* however, has been the inclusion of personal stories by people with mental illness, written in our own words and under our own bylines (often accompanied by a photograph of the contributor). A bold but necessary move, self-disclosure is a first step toward successfully addressing the stigma associated with being mentally ill. Before we can reveal ourselves to others, we have to come out of our own dark closets.

I strongly believe that recovery and empowerment are possible for everyone with a mental illness, which is why it is important for us to reach out to one another with information and strategies for coping in the world of the "normals." Whether working as corporate executives, bagging groceries in supermarkets, languishing on the back wards of state institutions, or sitting behind bars in cellblocks designated for the mentally ill, we find common ground, information, and empathy in *Voices.*

Readers also find tales to touch the heart—as when Pam Silvestri courageously told the story of her daughter Lisa, diagnosed manic-depressive and schizophrenic at the age of sixteen, who plunged to her death before reaching her twentieth birthday. On her final day of life, Lisa slipped away from the psychiatric hospital where she was a patient and took a train to visit an ex-patient friend. "My daughter had no psychiatric medications for several weeks," Pam wrote. "She must have thrown them down the toilet when no one was looking. . . . When she left her friend, she went back to the [train] station where witnesses said she was 'screaming, swerving and veering' on the platform. When an express train going north came through the station, Lisa vaulted in front of it to her death! Those dreaded voices urged her to leave this earth and her miserable existence!" And Lisa obeyed them.

After we published Pam's story, we heard from mothers and fathers who had also suffered the death, by suicide, of a child. Many broke their silence for the first time, thanking Pam for making it possible for them to speak now about what had previously been unspeakable. Far too often, friends of the family offer little solace around a self-imposed death, treating it as something shameful. Indeed, in certain religious communities, suicide *is* seen as sinful, with the result that surviving family members are abandoned not only by the deceased, but also by the same fellowship that would have rallied around if, say, the young person had been fatally hit by a truck.

What's unusual about these suicides is that there seems to be no sense to them, although there often are warning signs, including: a change in personality, isolation, extreme irritability, threats of self-harm, mutilation of parts of the body. To the parents who read Pam's article and called in because they feared that their sons and daughters might be suicidal, we offered the following advice:

- Take all *talk* of suicide, as well as even halfhearted attempts at self-destruction (scratching one's wrists, walking against traffic), seriously.

- Treat the problem as a real disease that requires immediate attention. Get the family member to a psychiatrist right away, and be careful about the person you choose. (I've learned that higher fees do not necessarily mean better-quality care.)

- Don't be ashamed—don't see this as a lack of character in your son or daughter . . . or in yourself. You're dealing with an illness. As you'd do with any other illness, obtain information on doctors, medicines, and treatment centers. Speak to friends. Check the Web sites of mental health organizations. Act now!

The newspaper began to receive so many requests for assistance from its readers that I introduced an Information and Referral Service (translation: a phone line in my home) to deal with them. And the calls came in! I would hear from people who had been denied Social Security benefits and needed to find free or low-cost legal services to handle their appeals. (So I had to learn about lawyers.) Other callers were seeking a doctor or therapist who would accept Medicaid. (I looked into doctors and social workers.) Some people asked about horticultural therapy and other programs that complement psychiatric treatment. In researching these and other queries, I was forced to broaden my network of people active in the mental health field. I met a lot of men and women who taught me a great deal.

Those who called in to the service were asked to get back to me if they didn't receive the information or help they needed from the referred party. I was becoming a walking encyclopedia of information both substantial and trivial. Sometimes, I'd find that my facts were incorrect, and I'd have to update my files. If necessary, I would advocate with the appropriate agency on a caller's behalf. "Yes, Mr. Steele," I began to hear time and again, as I reached people working in the vast bureaucracy of the systems that govern the welfare of the mentally ill. Yes, I was making a difference . . . and I drove myself even harder.

Not all requests to the Information and Referral Service were for help of a practical nature. Much that people shared was emotional for them (and for me), like a call I received one morning from a woman whose voice came haltingly across the line. "I won't have my brother, who is schizophrenic, visit our home for fear that he might harm my children, so he and I meet in restaurants or other neutral places," she said. "I know this hurts him, but don't I have to put my children's safety first?"

This one hit home, and I told her so. "Like you, my brother and his wife are uncomfortable around the family schizophrenic," I said. "I don't think they fear I will physically harm the children; there's no reason for them to do so, and yet they have decided to exclude me from their life. Yes, that hurts—just as I'm sure your brother is hurt by not seeing your children.

"On the other hand," I went on, "the good news is that you and he continue to meet. You haven't written him off."

"I'd never do that," she said.

"Great. Then make meetings between the two of you quality time," I said. "Let your brother know that you're available if he needs you. That may heal some of the hurt. Who knows? If you try to relax and enjoy your time together, you might discover that your fears are unfounded and that keeping him away from his nieces and nephews is unnecessary."

I felt encouraged by calls like this, for it meant that people were grappling with the issues and seeking guidance. It's misinformation and complacency that we need to worry about.

The phone kept ringing. More and more, I found myself getting wrapped up in other people's lives.

The voice that came over my answering machine one morning sounded female, soft, and urgent: "If you'd kindly put me on your subscription list and send me all the back issues, I'd be very grateful. I'm so lost. . . . It's not for me; it's for my son." The caller left an address and phone number.

I dialed the caller's number and reached a woman named Leora. "It's about Kevin," she said, "my son . . . an honor student at an elite university. At least, he used to be. One night a few months ago, Kevin arrived on our doorstep drugged, dazed, and catatonic. He'd left school, he told us, and then he refused to say another word. He didn't speak to us the next day or the next week. His father and I begged him to go for help, but Kevin wouldn't hear of it. Then one of his brothers asked him to see someone, and Kevin relented. The doctor told us our son was schizophrenic. She also said"—(and here Leora broke down)—"the doctor said, 'It's too bad he doesn't have cancer. That would be easier to cure.'"

Remembering that my own father and mother had once been advised to find an institution for me because, they were told, I would never get well, I found myself grieving with Leora—crying for her, for Kevin, for my parents, for the teenaged Ken, for all our pain, and for a dreadful diagnosis that fails to include the possibility of hope. But I knew better now, and so I asked Leora, "Where is your son?"

"He's here," she said. "He washes dishes in a diner, and then he comes home, talks to no one, and goes into his room. What do you think?"

"He's going to work every day," I pointed out. "That's positive."

We continued to talk for a while, and I told Leora to stay in touch. She did, with some frequency, for over a year.

One evening she called, sounding frantic. "I just overheard a conversation that Kevin was having with someone on the phone," she said, "and I don't know what to do about it."

"Tell me more," I said.

"He was talking to someone at an airline," said Leora. "I think he's planning to leave the country. I don't think we can let him go, but how do I stop him?"

"Does he have any money?"

"Just the little he's earned at work. I don't know if he can afford a ticket, but even if he can . . . there'll be nothing left for food and housing when he gets to where he's going. I don't believe Kevin would ever hurt anybody, but I think his judgment is so impaired that he'd be easy prey for anyone who wants to harm *him*. Ken, I fear for his *life*. Do I let him go, or do I call the authorities?"

I'm generally not in favor of putting anyone in a psychiatric hospital against his will, but Kevin was in danger. I knew full well that people suffering from mental illness are far more often the victims of violence than its perpetrators.

Leora had phoned me for support in making this most difficult of decisions, and I held her hand across the wire,
enabling her to call for help. Kicking and screaming, Kevin
was taken to a private psychiatric hospital, where he remained for several months. He's out now, seeing a therapist
and attending classes at a school near his home.

"Is he where I want him to be? Not yet," says his mother,
who has since become one of my very good friends. "But I
have hope now. And, on his good days, so does Kevin."

So do I.

As more people like Leora began turning to me for advice, I
realized I had to increase my knowledge of the things that
plague the mentally ill. The Ken Steele experience does not
stand for every schizophrenic experience, and schizophrenia
is not the only mental illness. Seeking other perspectives, I
surfed the Internet, where I was able to chat with others
attempting to meet the challenges of recovery. Soon I was
invited to write for several family and consumer Web sites,
and I became a featured contributor to the schizophrenia
home page (schizophrenia.com), where I posted my willingness to speak before groups.

Requests came in. I accepted invitations to address some
of the local affiliates of the National Alliance for the Mentally Ill, chapters of the National Mental Health Association,
and various other self-help organizations because I wanted
to spread the word about the Mental Health Voter Empowerment Project. To my surprise, however, people wanted to
hear more about my personal recovery story—probably
because I had met and conquered obstacles faced by many in
the audience, and I gave them hope. And so I began to tell

my story, over and over again. I spoke spontaneously, without notes. When I was done, members of the audience asked questions.

Among the questioners were mental health consumers:

Question: After years of being in the illness, I fear being able to cope with the world as a mentally well person. There are days when I'm tempted to stop taking my medication so I can return to a familiar, delusional world. Is it wrong to feel like this?

Response: No, it's natural. The so-called normal world presents many challenges to someone who has been out of it for a long time, and you worry whether you can meet those challenges. In a very true sense, it is the real world that now seems unsafe. I remember feeling terrified the day my voices stopped. I had lived with them for thirty-two years, and here I was, like Rip Van Winkle, waking up to a world that had greatly changed. And so had I. My decision was to take one day at a time, and that's my advice to you as well. Tell yourself: *I can stop taking the medicine and let the voices come back.* You have that power. But—and here's the important part—you also have the power to be well. Give sanity a chance. Believe me, it's worth it. And taking your medication is a small price to pay for it.

Question: I have been out of the illness for two years and feel that I'm cured of my disease. The doctors tell me that if I stop taking my medicine, the illness will return—hallucinations, confusion, paranoia, all of it. Do you agree?

Response: Emphatically, yes. Think of it this way: Just as a diabetic needs to take insulin to control diabetes, a schizophrenic must remain on medication—each and every day. It's a question of maintenance. Schizophrenia is a disease that *can* be controlled but not yet cured.

Question: Since becoming schizophrenic, I developed drug and alcohol problems. My parents won't let me come home because they say that my addictions—added to schizophrenia—make me more prone to commit violent acts. I tell them that the only person I'm liable to hurt is myself. Am I right?

Response: I understand why schizophrenics turn to drugs and alcohol in an attempt to mute the voices and illusions, but I don't condone it. I speak from experience. They only make things worse. But I think that's true in the general population as well. You introduce alcohol and illegal drugs into any group of people, with or without illness, and you automatically increase the possibility of violence occurring. It's not a mental health problem, it's a drug problem. You should educate your parents and other family members to this fact, but you need to be clean and sober first.

I heard from the families of mental health consumers:

Question: A family we know has a schizophrenic son, now middle-aged, who responded well to one of the new treatments, but his recovery completely upset the household. He's always been quiet. When he was in the illness, he heard voices, but they appeared to make him happy. He laughed and talked to them in whispers. He seemed content, in his own way. Since the voices went away, this same man has become very demanding. He wants to go out at night, to have a girlfriend, even to live on his own. Our son, too, is middle-aged and schizophrenic. We think he's too old to try these things, and we know *we're* too old to go through a delayed adolescence with him. Should we leave well enough alone or have him try one of the new medicines?

Response: I'll answer your question with a question: Whose life is it, anyway? Your son deserves the chance to make this choice *himself.* If he's able to achieve "wellness" and that would disturb the order of your home, have him move into a psychiatric residential program where he can take his first steps in a new life with help and support from people who are trained to manage these transitions. To sabotage his chance for recovery would be very, very wrong.

Question: Someone like you could not ever have been as sick as my son. You talk and make sense. He drools and can't manage his basic needs. Don't you think it is wrong to encourage people whose family members have no chance for recovery?

Response: I wouldn't have recovered if people hadn't taken a chance on me, if they didn't believe I could get well. I was one of those "no chance for recovery" folks you describe. If you can imagine me silent, I was . . . for almost a year and a half. And I was so sedated on one medication that the doctors misdiagnosed me as "catatonic" and prescribed tube feedings because I was so frail and thin. The drooling you talk about is likely a side effect of one of the older medications. For certain, the new atypical medications (risperidone, olanzapine, and clozapine) do not work for everyone, but take the chance. Encourage your family member to try them and *stay* on them for a while. Above all, don't give up.

I was invited to do grand rounds at various teaching hospitals, where I would speak to the concerns of professionals:

Question: In my practice, I frequently see patients who deny they are ill and won't take medication. How do I reach them?

Response: This is the question I'm asked most often by doctors, and it's the hardest to answer because it deals with relationships and attitude. Mental health professionals need to view the patient as part of the treatment process, not the patient as the object of the process. A patient who trusts a doctor, and who is trusted, is more likely to comply with a proposed plan of treatment. But I understand your frustration as a physician. Sometimes, the patient has to sink to the bottom before he decides that he doesn't want to drown and reaches for a lifeline. I hope you'll be there for him then.

When the meetings were over and the applause died down, I'd return to my apartment alone, exhausted, and afraid. In the back of my mind was the constant concern that I might revert to an old pattern of behavior: running away. In Westboro, in San Francisco, in Hawaii, wherever and whenever life seemed to be going well for me, for some strange reason I would feel threatened and I'd hit the road. I didn't want that to happen again. I needed somebody to hold *my* hand. I needed a support group.

And so I placed an ad in *New York City Voices*. It read:

AWAKENINGS: A New Approach to Self-Help

A new, peer-run support group, focusing on living successfully with schizophrenia and other psychotic mental illnesses, has begun on Manhattan's West Side. The group will meet on the second and fourth Tuesdays of each month, from 6:00–7:30 P.M. It will be led by Ken Steele.

People came—anywhere from six to seventeen at a given time. They crowded into the small front room of my apartment (where we still meet), seeking support in their efforts to make the transition from sick to sane. Things that most people pick up through life experience have to be taught to those of us whose primary residence, for years, has been our inner world. When we reenter "the real world," it's like stepping into foreign territory. We could do with the help of a guide or two.

Awakenings is unique. Where many other programs stress stabilization and maintenance for people whose illness is under control, our goal is full recovery. The point of these get-togethers is to enable members to talk to others who understand such things as what it's like to be interviewed for a job (the fears, the feelings) and then be rejected. Who understand the self-doubt that leads one to ask: *How do I adequately explain an absence of six months—or a year and a half—from the workplace?* Who understand when someone says, "I worry that people in my office are constantly gossiping about me." Who understand when a group member shares her ambivalence about telling her boss, or the people at work, that she suffers from a mental illness. (Although I favor self-disclosure, I know that employment discrimination is real and that people sometimes run the risk of losing their jobs when they reveal that they suffer from a mental illness. Sure, they can turn to the law in that case, but bringing a legal suit can be costly and time-consuming. To tell or not to tell? It's a personal decision.) Who understand when a member shares the following: "Although I've been stabilized on medication for six months, my parents still insist on knowing where I'm going when I leave the house, with whom, and when I plan to be back." (I counsel parents to cut their kids some slack. I understand that their concern comes from love and the experience of years of living with a mentally ill family member, but I also know that the recovery of that son or daughter, now an adult, depends on trust. We have to trust our young people to manage independence or they will never *become* independent.)

Hit and miss, out of need and invention, we were building an alternative system of our own: *by* mental health consumers and *for* mental health consumers. It was the Hawaii experience brought to the Big Apple (not just Manhattan, for a second group quickly formed in Brooklyn, and then a third and a fourth). The support group filled *my* immediate need just by their presence in my living room and my life. The more people on whom I depended and the more people who depended on me, I believed, the less likely it was that I'd skip out and run. However, the value of Awakenings went beyond this. It became an important source of material that enabled me to help other people through my columns, talks, and public appearances. I've always been in love with stories—hearing them, telling them. Real-life stories were now being used for real good things.

Requests for me to speak began to come in from around the country. In July 1996, I spoke about the Voter Empowerment Project at a plenary session of the National Mental Health Association in Washington, D.C. There I met Joe Glazer, president and CEO of the Mental Health Association in New York State. Joe is a strong advocate for the rights of mental health consumers, and he and I began to work together on several projects. In November 1998, I was elected to the organization's Board of Directors, becoming its vice chair of government affairs—the first consumer so designated.

Each step into the public spotlight provided me with exposure, and I welcomed the opportunity to spread the message that recovery from mental illness is possible and that people suffering from mental illness need to be understood and assisted, not feared and avoided. I grew used to being interviewed, to talking about voter empowerment, to telling my story in print, over the radio, and on television. And I knew that I *was* making a difference because of the response I received from readers and viewers.

On August 1, 1998, I was featured on "Four Stories," a television program that aired in New York and the tristate area over WNBC-TV. My phone number was shown on the screen. Less than a minute after the close of my segment, which lasted all of five minutes, my phone began to ring . . . and ring. By the time it stopped ringing, I had received close to

1,500 calls. These were new voices, too. I believed it was important to respond to each and every one of them.

I heard from teenagers and college students who had just begun to hear voices. Some didn't want to tell their parents. They didn't know what to do or where to go. After seeing "Four Stories," they felt that they could share their own stories with me. I encouraged them to speak to their parents at once and to get help.

Then there was a call from a mother with whom I spoke for close to an hour. She told me she had a nineteen-year-old son who she thought was a paranoid schizophrenic, and then she rambled on. Still, I listened. The conversation seemed to be going nowhere slowly when, as it came to a close, something extraordinary happened. The mother told me she had never taken her son to see a doctor. While she was at work or away from home, she would lock him in his bedroom to keep him safe.

"Why on earth hasn't he seen a doctor?" I asked.

"I've seen those movies about the mentally ill—*Asylum, Snake Pit, One Flew Over the Cuckoo's Nest*," she answered. "I know what happens in those places. I also heard you talk about the abuse you suffered in hospitals. I'll never let my son be placed in any of those institutions."

"How long has your son been ill?"

"Since 1994," she replied.

Her answer took my breath away. I encouraged her to seek help for her son—I even gave her names of several trustworthy doctors—and I told her that few people go to state hospitals nowadays.

"No," she said, remaining adamant. She knew what was best for her son.

We ended the call on a congenial note (I didn't want to alarm her), and I asked for her address so that I could send her some information. Then I phoned the local 911 number in her community and explained the situation. They'd take it from there.

A few days later, I received a phone call from relatives of the family; they expressed gratitude for my intervention. I had accomplished something they'd felt unable to do. They told me that the nineteen-year-old was in the hospital, receiving medication and responding well. The mother was angry and frightened but, in a way, also relieved and hopeful. The family had no idea of the gift they had given me with their call.

On January 30, 1999, a story about me—along with my photograph—appeared on the front page of the *New York Times*. Unlike other schizophrenics who make the front pages, I didn't have to kill anyone to get there. Reporter Erica Goode told of the cessation of my voices and the long climb back from schizophrenia's isolation, while highlighting the challenges before me, and others like me, to achieve lives of full independence. The *Times* article brought mail from people across the country. And when Dr. Seiden and I appeared on a *Voice of America* radio broadcast, we were contacted for information and help by families from eastern and western Europe, Africa, South America, Asia, and Australia—attesting to the fact that mental illness is no respecter of borders and boundaries. My message of hope, like a note enclosed in a bottle and cast out to sea, had reached shore and was being answered.

Miracles like this explain why I continue to do the work—even when exhaustion and physical ailments threaten to overwhelm me. As added inducement, I have but to look across my desk to the outer room, where Danny Frey is busily at work on the forthcoming issue of *New York City Voices*. At age twenty-four, Danny is the paper's managing editor, a frequent speaker and leader of workshops, and a recovering schizophrenic.

We were brought together through "Four Stories."

A handsome man with dark eyes and an easy smile, Danny grew up in the Bronx, attended a prestigious city high school, and enrolled in Lehman College. In his junior year, he started hearing voices. They said things to him like, *He's the man, He knows,* and *He's listening*. Danny took that as a sign that he was special. "I felt like I was inhaling spirits," he says. "It was a religious experience." He heard people talking to him from the radio and television. "I believed they had singled me out from all their listeners and viewers," he says, "because I was the only one brimming with energy."

Danny's father, Jacob, with whom he lived, noticed that his son was acting strange. One minute the young man would be chatting pleasantly; the next moment he might shout, "The force is with me." His schoolwork suffered. Like so many parents in this situation, the father tried to deny that anything serious was going on—until it was no longer possible to evade the truth. He asked Danny to go with him to the psychiatric emergency room at a local hospital "for a checkup." To the surprise of father and son, Danny was held for observation. He stayed in the hospital two weeks, was given Risperdal, then was discharged. But the dosage proved too high. The same high-energy kid who'd felt like a master of the universe began to complain of feeling sluggish. Unwilling to accept that he was mentally ill, he stopped taking his medication the day he got home. The symptoms returned at once.

"Four Stories" aired during Danny's second hospitalization, when his condition was deteriorating. Danny now refused to eat or take any medication, believing that people were trying to poison him. His delusions became more frequent and intense. Danny's father, his mother, Shulamit, and his younger sister, Sharon, grew desperate.

"Quick"—a family friend phoned Jacob one day while all this was going on—"turn on the TV. There's a man who's talking about having schizophrenia." Jacob caught the tag end of my story, took down the number, and phoned. He also brought a cassette tape of the show to Danny and played it for him in the hospital, to show him that recovery *is* possible. When Danny and I spoke a day or two later, I told him how important it was to stay on his medication (the dosage had been lowered). I also invited him to work with me on the newspaper when he felt well enough. Shortly thereafter, Danny showed up for work—and returned to school.

June 1, 2000: a sunny Thursday morning in the Bronx. I was seated at the crest of a grassy incline that overlooked South Field on the Lehman College campus, where row upon row of folding chairs had been set up facing a makeshift stage. Across from where I sat and at a somewhat higher placement from the field, elevated trains came and went with timetable frequency. The day was warm. All around me were hundreds of happy families—parents carrying flowers, grandparents being urged to find shade under trees or umbrellas to shield them from the blazing sun, laughing children clutching balloons that soared way over their heads. All were in their summer best, and everyone had a camera or camcorder at the ready as the music started up and the processional began.

This was the first college graduation I had ever attended. As I watched the proceedings, I thought for a few brief moments about all the opportunities that I'd been robbed of by my voices. How different my life would have been if I'd been able to finish high school, attend college, graduate, find a job, perhaps even marry and raise a family. But my feelings of regret were short-lived, for I quickly got caught up in the pageantry. First, the professors walked down in their varicolored robes, the different cowls and stripes signifying their degrees and the schools from which they'd received them. Then came the graduates in black gowns and tasseled mortarboards—long lines of beautiful young men and women, members of the first graduating class of the twenty-first century. I spotted Danny at once. He walked tall and straight, and he smiled.

A miracle, I remember thinking.

And I thought also: *There'll come a day when such miracles will be ordinary.*

I hoped I would live to see it.

When the ceremonies ended, we all posed for pictures, after which Daniel S. Frey, bachelor of arts, went off to lunch with family and friends.

"See you later?" I said as we parted.

"I'll be in the office this afternoon," he said.

And he was. After all, there was a newspaper to get out. And a lot more that needed to be done.

AFTERWORD

What Needs to Be Done

THE 1990s SPOKE to the possibility of better times for those of us who suffer from mental illness.

The good news: At the start of the decade, on July 26, 1990, President George Bush signed the Americans with Disabilities Act (ADA) into law. Proclaimed with great fanfare by the administration and received with great hope by the disabled community, the ADA attempted to level the playing field for people with physical and psychiatric disabilities so that they could compete with others who were not so challenged. The act's intent is to combat employment discrimination based on stigma and stereotypes. When informed that employees suffer from a particular illness, employers are expected to take "reasonable steps" to accommodate their needs in the workplace.

But: The ADA unfortunately has hurt many of those it was meant to protect because it requires disclosure of a condition before an accommodation can be made—and divulgence often leads to discrimination and dismissal. Emboldened by the law, Harold (a friend who worked for seven years as a research analyst at a Wall Street firm) approached his employer one day and shared information he'd long kept secret: that he suffers from manic depression with periods of paranoia. Because he has difficulty being around a lot of people, believing that they're talking about him, Harold requested a reasonable accommodation—moving to a quiet workstation in a less populated area of the office—so that he could better concentrate on his work. His request was granted, but his pleasure was short-lived. A few months later, Harold was part of a "downsizing"—the only one in his department to be let go.

Coincidence or discrimination in the workplace? I might have thought the former if I hadn't heard variations of Harold's story from many other men and women who bought the assurance of protection contained in the ADA's language and found that revealing their condition worked against them. Some of the best employees in America have been diagnosed with mental illness. They just haven't told their employers.

ADA is of little help to the majority of people who suffer from severe and persistent mental illness and who need treatment and support in order to enable them to even begin *thinking* about holding a job. Although the promise of the right to work is implicit in the act, the difficulty of accessing much-needed services stands as a major obstacle in reaching this goal.

The good news: Seeking to put teeth into the Americans with Disabilities Act of 1990, the Equal Employment Opportunity Commission (EEOC) issued "Guidelines on the American Disability Act and Psychiatric Disabilities" on March 25, 1997. The document gives employers detailed guidance about how to apply the policy already in place as a result of the ADA, explicitly including employees with mental illness. The guidelines seek to make clear to employers which psychiatric disabilities need to be accommodated and how to modify the workplace to meet the needs of someone with mental illness. For example, providing someone with a quiet work space, as was done for Harold, could be an easy and acceptable solution. Setting a flexible work schedule for an employee who is afraid to travel during rush hours might be another. Permitting frequent "refreshment breaks" for a person who suffers from dry mouth associated with taking certain medications would be a third.

But: Many people objected to the guidelines, citing as one of their reasons the potential for abuse. "Suppose that someone calls in sick, giving as an excuse that he is feeling depressed that morning," they said. "How does the employer know if the person is truly ill or just having a blue day?" Well, how do you know if any worker who calls in to say that he has the flu isn't actually off on a fishing trip? In fact, the "fishing trip" scenario is the more likely to happen. That's because the stigma attached to psychiatric disabilities is so strong that sufferers often go out of their way to hide their illness, to make it their business to show up for work so that no one can accuse them of slacking off. I know that from experience. When I broke my arm, I still made it to my transitional employment job every day. When I became afraid of taking public transportation, I got someone to accompany me to and from work. But I showed up at the office because, like so many others who suffer from mental illness, I was grateful for the work.

In many cases, the consideration we ask for is not special, but equal. A supervisor who identifies a worker as having a problem with alcohol or drugs will likely refer that person to the employee assistance program at the company, where counseling and treatment will be arranged. Employees with psychiatric problems should be dealt with similarly. Mental illness, if managed, should not preclude anyone from doing a good job. And involvement in satisfying work can be a major part of the healing process—as it's been for me and for millions like me.

The good news: On September 26, 1996, President Clinton signed into law the Federal Mental Health Parity Act of 1996 (one of the first major stories reported in *New York City Voices*). In simplest terms, parity seeks insurance coverage for mental disease that is on a par with that provided for physical disease. In April 1998, the act became the law of the land.

But: The federal plan is too limited. Although thirty-two states have implemented some form of parity, most restrict coverage to specific conditions—schizophrenia, major depression, bipolar disorder, schizoaffective disorder, and anxiety disorder—and most do not cover children (by virtue of the fact that these serious conditions tend to manifest themselves in late adolescence or adulthood). In one situation that I know of, Johnny, aged ten, was acting out in school. His condition was diagnosed as attention deficit disorder. Although his mother, a single parent, held a job and was insured through her employer, the policy did not cover Johnny's condition, so she had to pay for her son's doctor visits, counseling, and medication. If Johnny had been found to have asthma or juvenile diabetes, for example, his mother would not have had to take out loans in order to pay for his care. Insurance would have covered all or most of it.

Along with Doctors Molly Finnerty and Wilfred Noel Raby, I am one of the principal organizers of the National Picnic for Parity, begun in 1995 and since held every May in New York City. The event attracts as many as 10,000 people—picnickers as well as passersby whom we hope to educate about the importance of the issue. And it is this: The federal government must come up with a comprehensive parity law that requires insurance companies to provide the same level of mental health and substance abuse coverage that is offered for physical health care needs, and it must include a wide range of mental illnesses, not just those deemed the most severe. The argument I've heard raised most frequently against parity is its cost. I won't buy that. Not only is coverage for mental illness affordable, but it is a wise investment that will achieve long-term benefits for all our citizens. We can't afford to do without it.

The good news: On June 7, 1999, the first-ever White House Conference on Mental Health was convened at

Howard University in Washington, D.C. The conference brought together mental health consumers, advocates, researchers, and business and medical professionals to discuss mental health issues that affect 50 million Americans. Before an audience of 550 invited guests, plus individuals and groups participating via satellite links at nearly 6,000 sites across the country, conference leaders outlined steps to break down myths and misperceptions about mental illness; highlighted the fact that new medications were successfully treating psychotic illnesses, obsessive-compulsive disorders, and depression; and encouraged people to get the help they need. Public figures including Tipper Gore, who chaired the conference, and CBS's Mike Wallace shared their personal experience in dealing with depression and how they benefited from medical help, including medication. The conference's great strength was in countering the secrecy that too often surrounds the subject of mental illness and those who suffer from it.

But: The hard work begins where the conference left off. Combating the stigma of mental illness means reaching the mentally ill *first,* helping them know they are not alone, and giving them the courage to seek help. It also requires educating mainstream society, replacing misinformation (which can be scary) with facts (which can be encouraging). More conferences need to be scheduled, more frequently, at both national and local levels.

The good news: Another important step in the right direction was the first "Surgeon General's Report on Mental Health," a comprehensive document that was issued on

December 13, 1999. After noting that "22 percent of the population has a diagnosable mental disorder," Dr. David Satcher, the country's leading spokesperson on matters of public health, reported, "Nearly two-thirds of all people . . . do not seek treatment." The report is significant because it analyzes huge amounts of data and puts the government's stamp on what we know to be true: that mental illness is real, common, and treatable.

But: Will it take years for this report to make an impact, as was the case with an earlier surgeon general's report, on smoking, released in 1964? How many deaths from smoking might have been prevented had the public not taken thirty years to heed the wisdom in that report? How many suicides will take place before we listen to the warnings, and follow the advice, in this one?

The good news: On December 17, 1999, President Clinton signed the Ticket to Work and Work Incentives Improvement Act. This new law is the first major effort by Congress to end the unfair rules of the Social Security Administration, which prevented recipients of Supplemental Security Income and Social Security Disability Insurance (SSDI)—like my friend Peter—from continuing to receive essential medical benefits if they took a salaried job.

While living at a halfway house, Peter, a recovering schizophrenic, attended a clubhouse where he received training in word processing. Two years ago, Peter applied for a job as a word processor and was hired at a salary of $25,000 a year. Delighted at having a life, he began thinking about getting a place of his own someday. Everything now seemed possible.

Three months into the job, Peter received a letter from Social Security, asking him to come in. At the meeting, he was told that he was making too much money to qualify for SSI and receive Medicaid benefits. He hadn't expected to continue receiving the $600 monthly check for SSI (indeed, along with paying federal, state, and city taxes, he now paid money *into* the Social Security system), but he was greatly concerned about losing the Medicaid benefits that would cover the cost of doctor appointments and of the medications he needed to remain well. (Like me, he saw a psychiatrist who prescribed medicine as well as a therapist.) Medical insurance through his new company would not kick in until after he'd been on the job for six months, and then (he learned) he would not be covered for any preexisting conditions. And so Peter, who had become a contributor to society, quit his job and returned to being a recipient.

Under the new law, people with mental illness would be able to work, earn money, retain the Medicaid coverage that is essential to their maintenance and recovery, and pay their fair share of taxes. The incentive to have us work is just as much an incentive for America as it is for us!

But: We now need to implement the law in each and every state. That's a battle, as I and other advocates have discovered in my home state, New York, where nine participants in a public demonstration in favor of the Work and Wellness Act of 2000 were arrested. It's an uphill battle, and we cannot let up in our efforts to win it.

There is also a need for more training in employable skills so that when good jobs open up, we will be able to fill them.

The good news: The 1990s also saw the development of an array of effective medications to treat severe mental illness. New atypical antipsychotic medications like Clozaril, Risperdal, Zyprexa, and Seroquel, which reduce the terrible side effects of treatment, have now made it possible for growing numbers of people with schizophrenia and other mental illnesses to live successfully in the community. These successes go beyond mere symptom management. Many people have been able to launch new lives after decades of illness and institutionalization. For the newly diagnosed, like Danny Frey, medication and therapy have made possible a swift return to work and school. For their families, it's meant the difference between despair and hope. The possibilities for a successful future and full life are there.

But: Many of these new antipsychotic drugs are not covered by managed care companies because of their cost. As a result, people are still being given older medications, and many needlessly suffer the side effects: drooling, lethargy, a feeling of being sedated, or worse. I think of Suzanne, a vivacious young woman from California who was attending graduate school in New York when she had her first psychotic episode and was admitted to a psychiatric unit at a major hospital in the city. Shortly thereafter, I spoke with her parents, who had flown east to be with their daughter. They were shocked and worried, of course, but soon were heartened by Suzanne's positive response to one of the new antipsychotics. Still, they said, they'd be more comfortable if their daughter resumed her studies near home, so they could be there if she needed them. That seemed reasonable, and Suzanne transferred to a leading university in California. Despite the fact that Suzanne's illness was being successfully treated, the managed care company in California switched her prescription to a generic, less expensive medication. A month and a half later, Suzanne committed suicide. Cost cannot be a factor when prescribing the medication that is most likely to be of help in any given case.

Further, we need to launch a public relations campaign that will convince people to *stay* on their medications. At present, the best we can hope for is recovery, which is an ongoing process. Someday—in my lifetime, I hope—there will be a cure.

The good news: I do find a slight reduction in stigma against the mentally ill. When I saw my picture and story on the front page of the *New York Times* on January 30, 1999, I was elated—not because I was the person featured, but because a story about a schizophrenic who is using his time and energy in a constructive manner broke new ground. It made a positive statement.

But: For each such story, there are half a dozen others that report violent acts by schizophrenics and other mentally ill people—like Andrew Goldstein, who had a long record of aggressive behavior and an equally disturbing record of seeking help, asking to be hospitalized, and being turned away. At one point, according to records, he even requested eyeglasses so that he could find the people whose voices he heard talking to him. It took a fatal shove to finally get Andrew Goldstein the attention he required—and by that time, it was the wrong kind of attention. Headlines took over where help was required.

Stigmatization is the culprit here, and it is a public disgrace. It has to do with misinformation, ignorance, fear. We need to have people understand, not fear, our illness. Although some of the untreated mentally ill are dangerous, far more are harmless and are victimized by others. Their suffering is compounded by public ignorance and apathy. If someone falls down from a heart attack, people rush to help . . . perform CPR . . . call for an ambulance. If a person stumbles on the street, appears disoriented, and mumbles to himself, passersby give him a wide berth. The issue of stigmatization must be addressed. There are now far more mentally ill people in the nation's jails than in state hospitals—people arrested for shoplifting, intoxication, fare-beating, living on the streets. More than 300,000 mentally ill people are in our jails and prisons, five times as many as are being treated in our state hospitals. Many would never have been incarcerated if there had been adequate community caring . . . and care.

People with psychiatric illness belong in mainstream America. I live in a house that is not confined to the mentally ill; it has a general tenant roster, including the white-haired lady who greets me at the mailbox. I baby-sit for the kids of some of my neighbors. If you expect us to remain segregated—in housing, day treatment programs, menial jobs— you're going to get a continuation of the mental health community as a group apart. That benefits no one. You have to invite us in.

And make us feel welcome. Writing in the *New York Times* on November 14, 1999, reporter Erica Goode stated: "Perhaps the most difficult task facing the state is how to turn the mental health system into a resource that people will want to use. Mental health experts say it will require a fundamental shift in thinking such that the mentally ill are seen as people who matter, and who have the potential to recover, and eventually to work and to contribute."

At the beginning of the twenty-first century, I believe that this shift is taking place. Slowly.

I have a vision that goes like this: In this new century, mentally ill people will have the science, the organized voting strength, and the means to leave our ghettos of isolation behind us. We will finally join with the mainstream community, where we'll be able to live as independent individuals and not as a group of people who are known and feared by the names of our illness.

No buts about it.

Ken Steele died on October 7, 2000,
peacefully, in his own bed.
He would have been fifty-two on October 9th.

ACKNOWLEDGMENTS

DURING THE LAST WEEKS OF HIS LIFE, Ken Steele was engaged in the task of naming the men and women whose support and friendship he wished to acknowledge in this book. "There are so many people I want to thank," he would say when pressed to submit his list in order to meet our deadline. "I need more time so I can be sure that I've mentioned them all."

Time was one thing Ken did not have.

His record of those to be thanked, therefore, was left as a work in progress. And so, to the many of you whose names would have graced this page, please know that you were in Ken's heart . . . as he remains in yours.

As to my acknowledgments:

First and foremost, I am grateful to Ken for trusting me with his extraordinary life story. Recalling times that, in many cases, might have been best forgotten was not easy for Ken, but he persisted in the spirit of openness and honesty, two of his outstanding qualities. Ken was a class act, and I loved him.

Along the way, I was helped by many people—notably, Dr. Rita Seiden, a woman of wisdom and warmth. Steve Goldfinger, M.D., provided clarification as needed. So did Jennifer Heffron and Erica Malik of the National Mental Health Association. Danny Frey was there for me (and for Ken) in so many ways. Quietly and calmly, and always with a smile, Danny got things done. He is an extraordinary young man and a cherished friend.

Thanks, too, to the mental health consumers and their families who welcomed me to their gatherings and helped me feel at ease.

As Ken readily acknowledged, this book would not have happened without the tireless efforts of James Levine, our agent, who believed in the project from the start and supported both of us through its conclusion. That he brought Ken and me together with Jo Ann Miller, executive editor at Basic Books, was another stroke of fortune. Jo Ann is an editor who asks the right questions. I hope we have provided the right answers. Appreciation is extended, as well, to Jessica Callaway, her able assistant.

I am blessed with a supportive family. Noel Berman, my husband, not only gave me his love and understanding during sometimes difficult and, later, sad times, but also encouraged Ken during innumerable phone calls. Orin Berman, son and computer guru, saw me through many technological crises. To Eric Berman and Liz Umlas, Mitchell Berman and Ingrid Johansen goes my appreciation for their loving interest. Rachel Eliana and Jonah Adam are added to this list with my gratitude for the joy that they bring to my life today and the promise they hold for many tomorrows.

"Once upon a time there was a man named Ken Steele," I will tell them someday when they hold this book in their hands and are old enough to understand. "He was an American hero," I will say.

—*Claire Berman*